Carnegie Commission on Higher Education
Sponsored Research Reports

FROM BACKWATER TO MAINSTREAM:
A PROFILE OF CATHOLIC HIGHER
EDUCATION
Andrew M. Greeley

THE ECONOMICS OF THE MAJOR PRIVATE
UNIVERSITIES
William G. Bowen
(Out of print, but available from University Microfilms.)

ALTERNATIVE METHODS OF FEDERAL
FUNDING FOR HIGHER EDUCATION
Ron Wolk

INVENTORY OF CURRENT RESEARCH ON
HIGHER EDUCATION 1968
Dale M. Heckman and Warren Bryan Martin

THE FINANCE OF HIGHER EDUCATION
Howard R. Bowen
(Out of print, but available from University Microfilms.)

The following reprints and technical reports are available from the Carnegie Commission on Higher Education, 1947 Center Street, Berkeley, California 94704.

RESEARCH USE IN HIGHER EDUCATION: TRENDS IN OUTPUT AND INPUTS, 1930–1967, *by June O'Neill, published by Carnegie Commission, Berkeley, 1971 ($5.75).*

ACCELERATED PROGRAM OF MEDICAL EDUCATION, *by Mark S. Blumberg, reprinted from* JOURNAL OF MEDICAL EDUCATION, *vol. 46, no. 8, August 1971.*

SCIENTIFIC MANPOWER FOR 1970–1985, *by Allan M. Cartter, reprinted from* SCIENCE, *vol. 172, no. 3979, pp. 132–140, April 9, 1971.*

A NEW METHOD OF MEASURING STATES' HIGHER EDUCATION BURDEN, *by Neil Timm, reprinted from* THE JOURNAL OF HIGHER EDUCATION, *vol. 42, no. 1, pp. 27–33, January 1971.*

REGENT WATCHING, *by Earl F. Cheit, reprinted from* AGB REPORTS, *vol. 13, no. 6, pp. 4–13, March 1971.*

WHAT HAPPENS TO COLLEGE GENERATIONS POLITICALLY?, *by Seymour M. Lipset and Everett C. Ladd, Jr., reprinted from* THE PUBLIC INTEREST, *no. 24, Summer 1971.*

AMERICAN SOCIAL SCIENTISTS AND THE GROWTH OF CAMPUS POLITICAL ACTIVISM IN THE 1960s, *by Everett C. Ladd, Jr., and Seymour M. Lipset, reprinted from* SOCIAL SCIENCES INFORMATION, *vol. 10, no. 2, April 1971.*

THE POLITICS OF AMERICAN POLITICAL SCIENTISTS, *by Everett C. Ladd, Jr., and Seymour M. Lipset, reprinted from* PS, *vol. 4, no. 2, Spring 1971.*

THE DIVIDED PROFESSORIATE, *by Seymour M. Lipset and Everett C. Ladd, Jr., reprinted from* CHANGE, *vol. 3, no. 3, pp. 54–60, May 1971.*

JEWISH AND GENTILE ACADEMICS IN THE UNITED STATES: ACHIEVEMENTS, CULTURES AND POLITICS, *by Seymour M. Lipset and Everett C. Ladd, Jr., reprinted from* AMERICAN JEWISH YEAR BOOK, *1971.*

THE UNHOLY ALLIANCE AGAINST THE CAMPUS, *by Kenneth Keniston and Michael Lerner, reprinted from* NEW YORK TIMES MAGAZINE, *November 8, 1970 .*

PRECARIOUS PROFESSORS: NEW PATTERNS OF REPRESENTATION, *by Joseph W. Garbarino, reprinted from* INDUSTRIAL RELATIONS, *vol. 10, no. 1, February 1971.*

. . . AND WHAT PROFESSORS THINK: ABOUT STUDENT PROTEST AND MANNERS, MORALS, POLITICS, AND CHAOS ON THE CAMPUS, *by Seymour Martin Lipset and Everett Carll Ladd, Jr., reprinted from* PSYCHOLOGY TODAY, *November 1970. (Out of print.)**

DEMAND AND SUPPLY IN U.S. HIGHER EDUCATION: A PROGRESS REPORT, *by Roy Radner and Leonard S. Miller, reprinted from* AMERICAN ECONOMIC REVIEW, *May 1970. (Out of print.)**

RESOURCES FOR HIGHER EDUCATION: AN ECONOMIST'S VIEW, *by Theodore W. Schultz, reprinted from* JOURNAL OF POLITICAL ECONOMY, *vol. 76, no. 3, University of Chicago, May/June 1968. (Out of print.)**

INDUSTRIAL RELATIONS AND UNIVERSITY RELATIONS, *by Clark Kerr, reprinted from* PROCEEDINGS OF THE 21ST ANNUAL WINTER MEETING OF THE INDUSTRIAL RELATIONS RESEARCH ASSOCIATION, *pp. 15–25. (Out of print.)**

NEW CHALLENGES TO THE COLLEGE AND UNIVERSITY, *by Clark Kerr, reprinted from Kermit Gordon (ed.),* AGENDA FOR THE NATION, *The Brookings Institution, Washington, D.C., 1968. (Out of print.)**

PRESIDENTIAL DISCONTENT, *by Clark Kerr, reprinted from David C. Nichols (ed.),* PERSPECTIVES ON CAMPUS TENSIONS: PAPERS PREPARED FOR THE SPECIAL COMMITTEE ON CAMPUS TENSIONS, *American Council on Education, Washington, D.C., September 1970. (Out of print.)**

STUDENT PROTEST—AN INSTITUTIONAL AND NATIONAL PROFILE, *by Harold Hodgkinson, reprinted from* THE RECORD, *vol. 71, no. 4, May 1970. (Out of print.)**

WHAT'S BUGGING THE STUDENTS?, *by Kenneth Keniston, reprinted from* EDUCATIONAL RECORD, *American Council on Education, Washington, D.C., Spring 1970. (Out of print.)**

THE POLITICS OF ACADEMIA, *by Seymour Martin Lipset, reprinted from David C. Nichols (ed.),* PERSPECTIVES ON CAMPUS TENSIONS: PAPERS PREPARED FOR THE SPECIAL COMMITTEE ON CAMPUS TENSIONS, *American Council on Education, Washington, D.C., September 1970. (Out of print.)**

*The Commission's stock of this reprint has been exhausted.

Efficiency in Liberal Education

Efficiency in Liberal Education

A STUDY OF COMPARATIVE INSTRUCTIONAL COSTS
FOR DIFFERENT WAYS OF ORGANIZING
TEACHING-LEARNING IN A LIBERAL ARTS COLLEGE

by *Howard R. Bowen*

Chancellor, Claremont University Center

and *Gordon K. Douglass*

Professor of Economics, Pomona College

A Report Prepared for
The Macalester Foundation
and issued by
The Carnegie Commission on Higher Education

MCGRAW-HILL BOOK COMPANY
New York   St. Louis   San Francisco   Düsseldorf
London   Sydney   Toronto   Mexico   Panama
Johannesburg   Kuala Lumpur   Montreal
New Delhi   Rio de Janeiro   Singapore

The Carnegie Commission on Higher Education,
1947 Center Street, Berkeley, California 94704,
has issued this report as a part of a continuing
effort to obtain and present significant information
for public discussion. The views expressed are
those of the authors.

EFFICIENCY IN LIBERAL EDUCATION

A Study of Comparative Instructional Costs for Different
Ways of Organizing Teaching-Learning in a Liberal Arts College

Library of Congress catalog card number 79-167553

123456789MAMM7987654321

07-010034-9

Contents

Foreword

Today colleges and universities are pushed simultaneously toward costly change on the one hand and retrenchment on the other by concerned critics both on and off the campus. Some of these critics urge colleges to reform the instructional experience with enriched curricula and innovative teaching methods. Others warn the institutions against financial disaster and urge presidents to slash costs in every possible way. The Carnegie Commission on Higher Education will reflect both of these concerns in its forthcoming reports on academic reform and on effective use of resources in higher education.

In the meantime, we are impressed by the careful and challenging analysis of the efficiency of alternative instructional plans prepared, with support from the Macalester Foundation, by Howard R. Bowen and Gordon K. Douglass and reported in this volume. For the independent liberal arts colleges, at least, they demonstrate not only that changes in instructional modes are compatible with the efficient use of resources but that imaginative consideration of resource use may itself lead to instructional innovation and improved teaching and learning.

We wish to thank both the Macalester Foundation and the authors for the privilege of issuing their report as part of the Carnegie Commission's series of publications on higher education.

Clark Kerr
Chairman
The Carnegie Commission
on Higher Education

September 1971

Efficiency in
Liberal Education

1. *Introduction*

There are problems and weaknesses in the American higher educational system of 1970, but it can only be described as a thriving, going concern. Since 1955, enrollments have risen from 2,800,000 to 7,800,000, total expenditures have increased more than fivefold from $4.1 billion to $22.5 billion, and cost per student has risen from $929 to $1,865 (Table 1). Whereas in 1955–56 the expenditures of colleges and universities were 1.0 percent of the GNP, in 1969–70 they were 2.4 percent. This prosperity has resulted in the establishment of hundreds of new institutions, an enormous building program, and the raising of academic salaries to respectably competitive levels. It has also resulted in widespread extension of higher education to socioeconomic classes not previously participating and in notable improvements in the rigor and richness of the education provided.

During this great boom, the attention of faculties, administrators, and governing boards has been focused on growth and enrichment. In the past two years, however, it has become evident to all that the boom is slowing down. State legislatures have become increas-

TABLE 1 Trends in higher education	1955–56	1969–70	Projected, 1980–81
Total expenditures (billions of dollars)	4.1	22.5	39.0 *
Total expenditures as percent of GNP	1.0%	2.4%	2.8%
Enrollment (millions)	2.8	7.8	11.5
Educational and general expenditures per student (dollars)	929	1,865	2,852 *

*Assumes constant dollars after 1968–69.

SOURCE: Bowen, 1970, pp. 75–93, except estimates for 1969–70.

ingly resistant to the enormous annual increases in appropriations requested by public institutions, the federal government has been backing away from many of its programs involving support of higher education, and private donors have been hard pressed to maintain the rate of increase in gifts to which institutions have been accustomed. Moreover, student disorders and changes in campus life-style have alienated many members of the public and distracted the enormous public goodwill which colleges and universities had enjoyed during most of the 1960s. Many public officials and donors have begun to suggest that appropriations and gifts should be decreased, that tuitions should become the major source of income to institutions, and that students should be financed through long-term loans derived from the private capital market. The outcome of current economic and political forces appears likely to be a slowing down in the rate of increase in funds for higher education.

But the financial burdens of colleges and universities are still growing. Enrollments are likely to increase from 7,800,000 in 1969–70 to 11,500,000 in 1980–81, and expenditures to double (Table 1). The institutions are obliged to take on the terribly expensive task of educating millions of minority and other low-income students who need special educational services and vast amounts of financial aid. The institutions are equally obliged to offer new programs of education, research, and public service related to the pressing environmental, urban, and social problems of American society. Meanwhile, current and prospective increases in funds are being eaten away by inflation.

The net result of all these forces is financial stringency. This stringency is showing up in deficits in most private institutions and qualitative retrenchment in many private and state institutions. The current position of the higher educational community is agonizing. There is great danger that the hard-won gains of the past 15 years will be dissipated.

One approach to solving the problem is to improve the operating efficiency of colleges and universities. There are many allegations that higher education is ponderous, tradition-bound, unimaginative, and lacking in incentives to efficiency. Some observers hold that educational costs per student could be quickly reduced a quarter or even a half by applying the principles of business management. We have grave doubts about any such claims. Many of the allegations about inefficiency are based upon the narrow view that colleges and universities exist solely to give instruction, and that instruction should be organized like an assembly line. Few of the people making such assertions would send *their* children to the kinds of colleges they are recommending. At the same time, we believe that most colleges and universities have not had strong incentives to improve efficiency, that they are staunchly resistant to change, and that it might be possible over a period of years to offset a modest part of rising costs by improvements in efficiency. We believe, moreover, that these gains in cost effectiveness might be achieved without any sacrifice in standards and possibly with improvement in educational quality.

A country as rich as the United States and one so dependent on knowledge as its basic resource must give high priority to educational quality. It cannot afford to settle for less than genuine excellence, almost regardless of the cost. But it is at least possible that some qualitative progress can be achieved without commensurate increases in cost.

Efficiency is measured as a ratio between two variables: cost and output. An increase in efficiency occurs, for example, when output increases while cost remains constant. In the case of ordinary commodities such as wheat or electricity, output is quite easy to measure in terms of standard units (such as bushels or kilowatt hours), and cost per unit becomes an unambiguous measure of efficiency. But in the case of education, units of output are extraordinarily difficult to measure because each variation in cost may result in a qualitatively different output. One's estimate of efficiency, therefore, must be based on relatively subjective judgments about output. Merely because a given educational method results in lowered cost per student does not prove that it is more efficient unless it is agreed that there has been no qualitative deterioration of output (or at least a less than proportional qualitative deterioration). If one could measure efficiency only in terms of cost per student, as many observers seem to imply, there would be no difficulty whatever in improving efficiency. It would always be possible to spend less, and maximum efficiency would be reached at zero expenditures. The efficiency problem is to alter favorably the *ratio* of two variables, cost and quality. The best of all possible worlds exists when it is possible to cut cost and raise quality at the same time.

Sometimes it is argued that to raise educational efficiency one needs only to raise the teaching loads of professors. We do not deny that in certain isolated cases upward adjustments in teaching loads may be indicated. However, we believe that a preponderant majority of faculty members are working at full capacity in relation, for example, to the effort of comparable professional people and executives. We also believe that college professors have major responsibilities for scholarship, research, public service, and institutional service as well as for teaching, and that the success of their teaching in the long run depends on their participation in these other professional activities. Thus, while we intend to examine the effects of changes in teaching loads upon cost, we do not wish to propose academic "stretch-out" in which so-called efficiency is achieved by increasing the hours worked by the professor or by shifting some of his energies from research and service to instruction.

Then, too, we believe that good liberal education involves more than the transmission of facts and ideas of a kind that can be measured by test scores. It also involves outlooks, attitudes, values, motives, and development of character and personality. Therefore, it must include significant human and personal relationships between students and faculty and among students. We do not accept the notion that liberal education can be acquired by the accumulation of credits or can be conveyed wholly by mechanical or assembly-line techniques. Nevertheless, we believe that efficiency can be improved—improved without loading the professor unduly and without neglecting the personal aspects of good liberal education.

The purpose of this study is to explore the possibility of improving educational quality while reducing its cost. We believe that the higher educational community has a deep obligation at this time to be seriously concerned with efficiency not only as one promising line of attack on its financial problems but also as an essential step in winning the confidence of the American people.

This study was inspired by a memorandum entitled "Toward a System of Individually Taught Courses" (Appendix A) by Dr. Jarold Kieffer, a former professor of public affairs and administration at the University of Oregon. In this memorandum, Dr. Kieffer proposed that some or all of undergraduate instruction might be conducted individually, at each student's own pace, through the use of *learning stations* combined with general guidance and supervision of instruction. The learning station would provide the materials needed for each course, ranging from syllabi and readings to computer-assisted instruction, audio-visual aids, and laboratory equipment. Dr. Kieffer believed that this plan would result in improved instruction, possibly at reduced cost per student. He invited us to evaluate the plan with special attention to its cost. We then suggested that it might be useful to consider other possible modes of instruction in the same way and to produce a comparative study of the educational effectiveness and costs of several possible modes.

In this study, we examine six different modes of instruction. The Kieffer plan is one of them. We have chosen these six methods from among many possibilities because we believe each of them to be promising both educationally and economically. The sixth method, which we call the *eclectic model,* is an amalgam of the other methods, and constitutes our recommendation. We believe that a judicious combination of instructional methods is to be preferred to any one method applied uniformly throughout a college.

In conducting the study, we have been faced inescapably with the necessity of evaluating the quality or educational effectiveness of the several modes of instruction. We do not claim that our subjective judgments on this matter are above reproach. We have tried to describe each of the plans in sufficient detail so that any reader could make his own qualitative judgments—which may or may not agree with ours.

The study is confined to undergraduate instruction in small, independent liberal arts colleges. The results are suggestive for large universities and perhaps even for professional colleges, but we have made no attempt to extend the results beyond the independent liberal arts college.

Instructional costs at most colleges are about half their total budgets. In any broad-based exploration of efficiency, noninstructional costs must also be considered. We have devoted a brief passage to them in Chapter 6, but our primary concern throughout has remained with instructional efficiency.

The study centers on a hypothetical small liberal arts college of 1,200 students. This college operates with two conventional semesters of 16 weeks each. Students take as a full load four courses each semester. The range of subjects offered is comparable to that of most good liberal arts colleges, including the major fields of natural sciences, social sciences, and humanities. Most courses are offered only once a year but are repeated every year. Faculty members are allowed sabbatical leaves after six years of continuous full-time service; the leave is one semester at full pay or one year at half pay. Compensation to faculty and staff (with respect to salary and fringe benefits) and the distribution of faculty by ranks are comparable to those found in actual well-known colleges. In short, we have used as a frame of reference a small liberal arts college of better than average quality. We examine the effect upon cost of variations in mode of instruction within such an institution.

If a change in the mode of instruction is to affect cost, it will ordinarily do so by changing inputs in one or more of the following ways:

1 It may substitute low-cost labor for high-cost labor, e.g., by replacing faculty time with assistant time or by increasing the proportion of junior members in the faculty.

2 It may increase intensity of labor usage, e.g., by raising teaching loads for faculty.

3 It may substitute student initiative for faculty supervision, e.g., by making study more independent.

4 It may substitute capital for labor, e.g., by using the library or television in place of lectures.

5 It may intensify utilization of capital, e.g., by using buildings and equipment more fully.

6 It may substitute low-cost capital for high-cost capital, e.g., by employing temporary buildings, reducing standards of construction, or cutting down on expensive library acquisitions.

7 It may change curricular mix, e.g., by increasing enrollment in low-cost subjects (sociology) and by reducing it in high-cost subjects (physics).

8 It may reduce noninstructional services.

9 It may spread overhead costs by increasing the scale of operation.

The modes of instruction examined in this study will involve some of these changes in inputs.

2. Modes of Instruction

Five of the six modes of instruction which will be investigated in this study are described in this chapter. They include what we have chosen to call a *conventional plan,* variations of which are in use at most small independent liberal arts colleges; a modified version of the *Ruml plan,* featuring a few large lecture courses; an *independent study plan,* which puts major learning responsibilities upon students; a *tutorial plan* designed by David Bakan; and a plan of individual instruction linked to modern teaching-learning equipment, referred to in this study as the *Kieffer plan.* A sixth mode of instruction of our design, called the *eclectic plan,* will be introduced and evaluated in Chapter 5.

CONVEN-TIONAL PLAN The curricula of most small independent liberal arts colleges are being taught today much as in past decades, that is to say, by instructors giving lectures and leading discussions on aspects of a discipline, usually to a small group of students (in the range of eight to forty) who follow a common course outline, read the same or similar books, often write related papers, take identical quizzes and examinations, and meet regularly and frequently in a classroom throughout the semester. Laboratory work in the sciences and languages and studio work in the fine arts complement these lecture-discussion courses.

Some private colleges, of course, already have broken with conventional modes and have adopted dramatically new "experimental" methods of instruction in all or most of their curricula. Many others have introduced honors programs, tutorials, "reading and research" courses, work internships, semester-abroad programs, calendar changes, and other innovations in some fields or some courses. Even so, conventional plans of instruction, in various incarnations, are very widespread indeed and deserve our first attention.

A conventional plan combines labor and capital of particular sorts in unique ways to "produce" the outputs of higher education. The labor that is used to staff a conventional plan, for example, is "high-priced" labor in the sense that fully qualified professionals, rather than technical assistants or students (as in independent study), make up the work force. In a conventional plan instructors are expected to teach and students to learn. Students play a relatively passive role in such courses except during programmed discussion periods and, in the case of laboratory and studio courses, during some periods of observation, practice, and experimentation. Laboratory assistants may be used in the sciences to set up demonstrations and supervise labs, but, outside the sciences, teaching or grading assistance is rare.

The *intensity* with which a conventional plan uses labor is less clear than its average price. On the one hand, instructors of conventional courses tend to teach more classes per year than they would in some instructional modes. Apart from scientists, whose responsibilities for laboratory instruction lengthen their time commitments per course, most instructors teach five or six classes per year under a conventional plan. Other plans, notably those of Bakan and Kieffer (to be described subsequently), program lower teaching loads. Average class size in a conventional plan, on the other hand, is considerably lower than in several plans, especially those of Kieffer and Ruml. One reason for this is the readiness of faculty in a conventional plan to section courses with large enrollments into two or more "normally" sized classes. On balance, a conventional plan causes instructors to teach more classes but fewer students per class than some of the other plans and therefore probably is in an intermediate range of labor "productivity."

The capital required to implement a conventional plan varies widely from field to field, but in no case does it seem to be viewed as a substitute for labor. Physics, chemistry, biology, and music all require heavy investments in specialized equipment, as to a lesser extent do art, theater, psychology, and languages. Most fields require access to a decent library collection, and some lean heavily upon modern computer facilities. Classrooms, studios, laboratories, and auditoriums of various shapes and sizes also must be provided, though perhaps not so generously or so lavishly as they are on many campuses. But a conventional plan of instruction tends not to use even old-fashioned kinds of audio-visual equipment extensively, not to mention newer instructional devices such as computers.

This analysis suggests that the costs of producing a unit of educational output in conventional ways probably are moderately high. Professionally trained labor, the primary input, is costly; it is used in only moderately intensive ways; and it is combined with relatively expensive capital inputs, some of which lie idle much of the time.

Some sense of the *quality* of instruction produced by a conventional plan may be gleaned from the mountains of recent literature describing alternative reform proposals. The conventional plan has been criticized most frequently for its failure to give students responsibility for their own education, and for its imposition on students of educationally inefficient time budgets. Either shortcoming could influence the quality of instructional outputs by undermining the incentive and capacity to learn.

The conventional plan of lecture-discussion courses, it is argued, confronts students with predesigned syllabi, packaged lectures, detailed assignments in textbooks, frequent quizzes, and the like, leaving them little incentive to discover how to learn by themselves. These characteristics act as factorylike pacing devices, moving students over a series of arbitrarily established time-hurdles toward the completion of a "course" and a semester so that they may move on to other courses and other semesters. In such a system, many believe, the tendency of students to cram knowledge, regurgitate it, and forget it is high. What is needed, they maintain, is some form of independent study where learning for its own sake takes place outside the conventional pattern.

The conventional plan also tends to fragment students' time and attention. A typical student's program is a semester-long series of often unrelated 50-minute classes distributed unevenly in time. Somehow he must distill from a day's or a week's series of disparate presentations those bits and pieces which give continuity to each subject. He rarely is permitted to direct his efforts selectively, taking certain related courses in direct succession or simultaneously in clusters so as to maximize learning momentum. Nor is he normally allowed to speed up or slow down from the pace of the rest of a class to allow for his special starting point and capacity. Instead, a uniform pace is determined by the instructor, based somehow on his sense of class capacity to make collective progress, leaving good students bored and slower students anxious. Again, the most common remedy proposed is some kind of independent or individualized study.

This sample of frequent criticisms hints strongly that the conventional plan of instruction may produce educational outputs which not only are costly but also lack high quality.

THE RUML PLAN In 1959, Beardsley Ruml wrote a little book, *Memo to a College Trustee,* outlining some of the ways he believed instructional operations in liberal arts colleges might be made more efficient. One of his proposals is that the size distribution of classes be changed. Writing when interest in general education courses was still keen, he proposed the inclusion of several very large lecture courses in the schedule of classes each semester, along with the more traditional lecture-discussion and seminar offerings. Under his plan, students might take a quarter of their work each semester in a large but qualitatively excellent course central to the college curriculum, instead of picking and choosing among a variety of smaller (and qualitatively inferior) courses for that part of their work. Adopting the Ruml plan could reduce the curricular offerings of a conventional plan by almost a quarter, he thought, yielding substantial savings.

The arithmetic of Rumlizing some classes is straightforward. In a college of 1,200 students, each taking four courses per semester, the number of student course registrations each term is 4,800. Four large lecture courses, each designed to cater to the general education needs of a particular level of students, might absorb 1,200 or one-fourth of these registrations, averaging 300 students per course. Had these registrations been distributed among normally sized classes of 20 students each, 60 different classes would need to be staffed. Thus, introduction of four large lecture courses each semester would permit a net reduction of 56 courses.

The essence of Mr. Ruml's idea is the boosting of labor "productivity" above conventional plan levels. Even if the teaching loads of instructors who staff large lecture courses were greatly reduced to permit careful preparations—reduced to one course per instructor per term, for example—higher enrollments per course would more than offset the effect on labor utilization of reduced loads. Again, arithmetic shows the difference: Whereas before, 60 courses were staffed by the equivalent of 24 instructors (each teaching $2\frac{1}{2}$ courses per semester), four large lecture courses would require only four instructors, each devoting full time to his course; whereas course enrollments per instructor formerly amounted to 50 on the average, large lectures would boost the average to 300.

Ruml recommended that each college assign its best talent to these courses, and if necessary pay handsome salaries to attract professors able to teach large courses effectively. The need to supply each instructor of a large lecture course with special assistants for grading papers and examinations, etc., would raise input prices even higher for each unit of labor. But the number of (high-priced) labor units required would be greatly reduced, producing substantial savings in the salary budget.

Capital costs also should be lower than normal under the Ruml plan. One reason to expect lower capital costs is that space needs per student in large lecture halls are considerably lower than in small classrooms. Another reason is the effect of large lecture courses on library needs: because students in large lecture courses use common syllabi, the number of library volumes required to service their reading needs should be lower and the utilization of existing book stocks should be higher than for a conventional plan.

The net effect of these changes in productivity and input prices should be to lower costs per unit of instructional output. Higher prices of labor inputs would be more than offset by higher rates of labor utilization under the Ruml plan, and lower capital costs would reinforce the potential savings of labor.

What would happen to the quality of instruction under the Ruml plan is unclear. On the one hand, Ruml claimed that quality should rise if colleges were to take seriously his plea that the ablest instructors be assigned to large lecture courses and that they be given the time, equipment, and assistance necessary to do their best jobs. Also, a substantial body of evidence denies that there are significant qualitative differences among various modes of instruction. But there is also a long list of complaints about large classes, based mostly upon the experiences of students at large universities. These complaints differ little from those leveled at the conventional plan: large classes discourage learning for its own sake; they seal students into academic locksteps and make discussion and personal encounter impossible.

PROGRAMMED INDEPENDENT STUDY   Programmed independent study has been proposed as a means of meeting some of the objections to the conventional plan of instruction enumerated above. Unlike the usual independent study course under which each student pursues a unique or tailor-made program, this plan calls for a carefully devised program which would be followed by many students on roughly the same time schedule. The program would be outlined initially in a syllabus which suggests readings, assigns papers and problems, and schedules examinations. At an initial meeting, the instructor of each course would make clear, however, that within the broad framework of the course, each student would have considerable latitude to pursue his own interests through research and original writing. Students would be free to consult the instructor individually about their projects, and the instructor would meet from time to time with the entire class for discussion. But the course would be managed so that the instructor would spend less time in all the course's activities than he ordinarily would spend on a conventional course. Students themselves would replace the instructor as the sources of some inputs.

This plan could be combined with supervised laboratory instruction, or it could include some activity at "learning stations" where mechanized learning aids would be available. With these modifications, the plan would be adaptable to most subjects. Even so, the plan is not proposed for the entire curriculum; rather, it is seen as a substitute for one-fourth to one-half of the courses provided by the conventional plan.

Programmed independent study, like the Ruml plan, would harvest savings primarily by reducing the amount of instructor labor used in the educational process (per course). So long as students and instructors alike would discipline themselves to husband instructors' time, the time saved by the plan could be spent by assigning more courses (but not heavier work loads) to instructors. In this way, the same number of courses could be offered students by fewer numbers of faculty, and the costs per course might be reduced.

Capital costs might also change under this plan. One visible economy would be the cost of classroom use, which should fall considerably below that of the conventional plan because formal class meetings would be less frequent. The costs of providing additional library and computer services to independent study students might climb, on the other hand.

The plan's chief selling point is not its cost-saving ability, however, but its potential for raising the quality of instruction. It is based on a theory of education that calls for each student to follow his interests and curiosity and to be an active pursuer of knowledge rather than a passive receptacle and a follower of instructions. By increasing the initiative and self-reliance of students, the capacity to learn also should increase, augmenting instructional outputs through "learning by doing." If the plan is to work, on the other hand, those students who are unable to take responsibility for their own instruction would fail. The program quickly would lose its educational effectiveness and its economy if an effort were made to carry such students along under the close guidance of the instructor.

THE BAKAN PLAN

The essence of this instructional mode, which has been proposed by Professor David Bakan of York University in Canada (see Appendix D), is a highly compressed and relatively unstructured curriculum accompanied by an extensive use of tutorials. The main purpose of the plan would be to arrange the instructional system so that the tutorial method could be used without undue cost. Under the Bakan plan, each student would be free to elect from a list of courses being offered whatever courses he was qualified to enter, and, with the instructor of each of his courses, he would develop an individualized study plan at the beginning of each term. Normally he would enroll in four courses per semester during the freshman and sophomore years and three per semester during the junior and senior years. Instructors would be free to offer whatever courses they wished and to teach as they saw fit, but relative independence of study would be encouraged. They could meet their classes formally one, two, or three times a week—or not at all, and they would meet their students individually in tutorials at least three times during a semester. The three required tutorials would be for the purposes of agreeing on course assignments and requirements, reviewing students' progress, and evaluating their accomplishments.

The following table describes in greater detail how a typical instructor teaching two courses per semester might budget his time to accommodate the style of the Bakan plan[1]:

Option A

Hour-long individual tutorials	4½ per student	180
Class lecture-discussions	6 hr per week	90
Preparations, etc.	14 hr per week	210
	Total hours per semester	480

[1] It is assumed in this table that instructors might reasonably be expected to devote 30 hours a week during the 16 weeks of a semester to instruction.

Option B

Hour-long individual tutorials	6 per student	240
Class lecture-discussions	4 hr per week	60
Preparations, etc.	12 hr per week	180
	Total hours per semester	480

Option C

Hour-long individual tutorials	7½ per student	300
Class lecture-discussions	2 hr per week	30
Preparations, etc.	10 hr per week	150
	Total hours per semester	480

The number of tutorials for each student could be greatly increased if more than one student attended each tutorial session or if the sessions were reduced in length to 45 or even 30 minutes. For example, under Option C, if two students attended tutorials lasting 45 minutes each, the number of tutorials per student would rise from 7½ to 20, or more than one a week throughout the semester.

In a college of 1,200 students and 100 faculty members, 200 courses could be offered each semester with average enrollments of 20 students each. This compares with an offering of 250 courses per semester with 2½ course loads for instructors under the conventional plan—a relatively modest compression of the curriculum in order to accommodate tutorial instruction.

The interesting feature of the Bakan plan is that it demonstrates the feasibility of incorporating tutorial instruction into a college program without raising the work load of instructors—assuming that 30 hours a week during the academic year is a reasonable amount of time for a faculty member to devote to instruction (see Chapter 3 for a discussion of faculty work load).

From the point of view of efficiency, the Bakan plan would not reduce instructional costs, but neither would it necessarily raise them. The most striking difference between it and the Ruml or programmed independent study plans is the fact that the latter plans would raise faculty productivity as compared to the conventional plan while the Bakan plan would lower it. In order to serve students more intensively in tutorials, instructors would be permitted lower teaching loads unaccompanied by increased class sizes. The effect of this fact on costs could, however, be counteracted by a constriction of the curriculum, and this, indeed, is what Professor Bakan proposes. Another effect of limiting the number of courses offered would be the surrender by students of some breadth of choice in course selection. Capital costs probably would move downward because of less frequent use of classrooms, upward because of greater use of library and computer facilities.

Students would likely react to tutorial instruction differently. Some, whose initial level of competence and confidence are high and whose earlier experiences with independent study were rewarding, would profit greatly from the Bakan plan and endorse its introduction enthusiastically. For them, the quality of instructional outputs would almost certainly rise. Others, more timid, less experienced, and not so far along in gaining command of a subject area, would find tutorials frustrating and less productive than more passive learning modes. Predicting with any degree of accuracy how output quality would be affected by individual tutorials, therefore, is virtually impossible. Professor Bakan's claim that his plan would improve instructional quality because it would encourage teachers to teach what they want and are competent to teach rests on a presumption that teachers of conventional courses frequently are denied their preferences of course assignment. The reader must be the judge of whether this presumption is valid. Since the Bakan plan would be less likely to produce a balanced set of courses for students to choose among—unbalanced at least in the sense a conventional curriculum provides breadth of coverage—the reader also will have to decide whether traditional curricular structures or Bakan-induced structures would be more likely to create among students the intellectual and emotional capacities needed for access to new knowledge.

THE KIEFFER PLAN   This mode of instruction, described by Jarold Kieffer in the memorandum "Toward a System of Individually Taught Courses" (see Appendixes A and B), calls for the creation of courses in which, with the assistance of modern teaching-learning equipment and willing instructors, students might study at their own convenience and at their own pace. Each course would have a program organized in sequential phases. The program would consist of instructions, reading assignments, problems, use of audio-visual materials when relevant, laboratory tasks, witnessing demonstrations, making certain field trips, etc. For some courses, e.g., laboratory science courses, procedures might differ little from conventional course work. For others, e.g., English literature or history, the program would consist primarily of reading, problem solving, and writing, and might be centered at the library. For many courses, however, special "learning stations" would be provided where programmed course materials would be available. Some of them might be retrieved electronically from a central course materials "bank." At these stations students individually could view and hear materials continuously, in segments, or repeatedly through manipulation of simple controls.

For a typical course, each student would come at his convenience to a learning station (or library or laboratory if that were the station) and work on the program for phase I of the course at his own pace. At the completion of the phase he would attend, along with other students at the same state of readiness, a seminar with the course instructor. Each seminar would provide informal discussion, opportunities for questions, answers, and additional perspective. After this, if the student judged he was ready, he would take a test. If he passed the test, he would proceed to phase II, etc. If he failed he would return to phase I with no penalty other than delay to repair his deficiencies. A comprehensive examination after successful completion of all phases would be the basis of the course grade, though the results of reports, reading, term papers, etc., could also be counted. The student would be free at any time during the course to consult his instructor privately, but their primary contact would be in seminars and indirectly at learning stations where programmed learning materials would bear the unmistakable mark of each instructor.

The Kieffer plan, like the preceding two plans, is based on independent study. It differs from other plans in three important and related respects, however.

The first difference is the heavy commitment of time each Kieffer plan instructor must make in preparing, updating, and improving programs well in advance of making them available to students. During this period of time the instructor, perhaps with the help of a psychologist experienced in learning behavior and an audiovisual specialist, would select the kinds of knowledge and experiences he wanted students to have on completion of each phase, choose the methods of presenting each part, produce or assemble necessary materials such as video film sequences, and perhaps test critical materials for effectiveness on student volunteers.

Mr. Kieffer estimates that program development alone might take up to a year of staff participation per course.

The second difference, a corollary of the first, consists of "software" packages, especially the programmed materials committed to videotapes, produced for Kieffer plan courses. These might be produced locally in campus studio facilities with altogether "native" resources, or they might be produced cooperatively by several institutions or by commercial companies. In either case, the finished product would result from numerous technical inputs and would require specialized equipment to display it.

Finally, the Kieffer plan differs from other independent study schemes by requiring major investments in audio-visual storage, control, and playback equipment. Its sophistication, however, could vary from highly complex and expensive to relatively simple and cheap. If the amount of hardware and programs were relatively simple, the Kieffer plan could merge into the Bakan or programmed independent study plans described above.

All three of these differences suggest that inputs of capital bulk large in Kieffer plan instruction. The time taken by instructors, psychologists, and audio-visual technicians to create a course's programmed software is valuable in the same way that its complementary hardware is valuable to the creation of instructional outputs: both kinds of capital investments serve as basic inputs into the educational process. The returns from these investments would continue for a number of years, the exact number depending upon the life of the software and hardware, respectively. It is reasonable to suppose that the costs of creating these capital assets in the first place, then, ought to be spread equitably over their useful lives.

The Kieffer plan's costs compared to conventional plans would depend primarily upon the unit prices of these capital inputs (best expressed perhaps as a rental value per year), the unit prices of labor inputs they may replace, and the degree to which capital actually substitutes for labor in educational production under the Kieffer plan.

With respect to hardware costs, our investigations have convinced us that implementation of the Kieffer plan would commit even small colleges to large investments in high-priced teaching-learning equipment. Lower-priced units, e.g., video-cartridge recorders, at present levels of quality and reliability, would be inadequate substitutes for more expensive reel-to-reel equipment. The national engineering press recently has forecast major technological advances in cartridge systems which could, in time, alter hardware costs. But until the state of the art changes and prices drop dramatically, capital costs for the Kieffer plan would remain high.

Software costs, on the other hand, would vary so widely from course to course that little can be said about relative prices of this important input of the Kieffer plan. Perhaps the most dramatic way to lower software prices would be to standardize course development on an interinstitutional or national basis, thereby spreading development costs over many more units of instructional services. Unlike hardware systems whose technical characteristics virtually forbid interinstitutional cost-sharing arrangements, programmed learning materials easily could be developed cooperatively. The one drawback of such arrangements would be the denial to individual instructors of latitude and individual creativity in the selection of objectives and material for their courses.

The primary source of efficiency gain in the Kieffer plan is labor saving in the actual conduct of courses. Instructors would meet their students in occasional seminars to discuss the materials of each phase, and they would see students in need of special assistance individually. The seminars at the end of each phase, moreover, would have to be repeated a second and perhaps a third time to accommodate the different speeds at which students would progress through the course. But preparations for seminars would be light for most instructors, and the grading of examinations at the end of each phase could be delegated to learning stations (with the use of programmed testing devices) or to student assistants. These savings of instruction time should permit a substantial increase in the average enrollment per course without placing inordinate additional burdens on instructors. They should not be used to multiply the number of Kieffer plan courses, however, because of the heavy involvement of instructors in program development and updating.

If our estimates of the time required to conduct Kieffer plan courses are roughly correct, then introduction of the Kieffer system might lead to both labor saving (by capital substitution) and increased labor productivity. In other words, capital costs per student enrollment undoubtedly would rise, but these increases in cost would be offset at least partially by reduced labor costs per student enrollment. Our judgment, in the present state of the technical arts, is that the former effect on costs would outweigh the latter, and therefore, that the Kieffer plan would be relatively costly.

The chief virtue of the Kieffer plan, in our view, is that it attempts to overcome the faults of the conventional plan in a direct and forthright way. It acknowledges more directly than other plans the need to make whole the traditionally fragmented time budgets of students. It permits students to set their own pace and to choose their best times for concentrated study. It also provides them with a vehicle of instruction which is designed to maximize learning momentum. The purpose of programmed instruction, according to Mr. Kieffer, is to force instructors to specify the kinds of results they wish to achieve *before* selecting modes and materials; in this way, he thinks the parts of a course would become much more integrated, more cumulative, and students who take the course would see more quickly the interrelationships among materials and learn better how to manipulate information for new meaning.

The Kieffer plan also attempts, but less directly, to teach students how to learn on their own initiative. It is likely to do less well in this regard than the programmed independent study plan and perhaps the Bakan plan, however, because the materials for study are so rigidly programmed. Unless the programmed materials are supplemented in a major way with open-ended assignments, requiring students to fend for themselves as in true independent study, the Kieffer plan really does not meet fully the most telling criticism of the conventional plan, namely, that the latter saps initiative and encourages passivity among students. From the point of view of cost efficiency, adaptation of the Kieffer plan to increase individual initiative would substantially increase the time commitment of course instructors to student counseling and paper grading and take away much of the potential gain in labor productivity identified above.

Even so, the Kieffer plan strikes us as one which would raise the quality of instructional outputs very significantly.

SUMMARY AND CONCLUSIONS Table 2 summarizes in a rough and ready way the chief findings of this chapter. In it we have compared instructional modes as economists tend to view them, viz., as processes of production which transform inputs of labor and capital into outputs of instructional services.

TABLE 2
Relative costs of selected instructional modes

Mode of instruction	Prices of inputs		Degree of labor intensity* (3)
	Labor (1)	Capital (2)	
Conventional plan	high	moderate	high
Ruml plan	very high	moderate	high
Programmed independent study	high	moderate	moderate
Bakan plan	high	moderate	high
Kieffer plan	high	hardware: high; software: high to low; other: moderate	moderate

*Relative importance of labor in the production of instructional outputs.

†Units of instructional services produced per unit of labor input.

One interesting feature of the table, revealed in its first two columns, is the rather narrow range of price variations for necessary inputs among the plans. Such narrowness may reveal only the biases of the authors. But we are inclined to believe that it also represents a widespread view among the faculties and administrations of small independent liberal arts colleges that little could be gained and much harm might come from attemping to substitute cheaper for dearer labor or capital. On the labor side, these colleges regard, say, the hiring of teaching assistants to replace full-time, fully qualified instructors as not only an invitation to lower-quality instructional outputs, but also a way to rob colleges of a feature which helps to distinguish their teaching methods from most undergraduate instruction at large state universities and colleges. The price of capital inputs, too, is narrowly viewed. The principal reason for this, we suspect, is the quaint way most colleges keep their books, never allocating to instructional costs an appropriate share of the costs of plant and equipment.

Another similarity among plans is the relatively high degree of labor intensity revealed in column (3). Education is a labor-intensive business, requiring for its production much labor compared to other inputs including capital. Only the programmed indepen-

Relative labor productivity† (4)	Relative costs of outputs (5)	Relative quality of outputs (6)
moderate	moderately high	moderate
very high	moderately low	moderate
high	moderate	moderately high
moderately low	high	moderately high
high	high to very high	moderately high

dent study plan and the Kieffer plan are shown to be moderately rather than highly labor-intensive, and the reason for this is, in the first instance, the importance of student initiative in independent study, and, in the second, the fact that a major share of labor time was capitalized in order to spread the costs of course preparation across several years of use.

Column (4) tells the major difference between plans. The range of labor productivities revealed here is from moderately low to very high—from an extremely low student load per instructor to a very high one. The size of classes and the number of classes taught by faculty combine to produce these differences. On these grounds, the Ruml, programmed independent study, and Kieffer plans stand out as the most efficient modes of instruction.

Finally, columns (5) and (6) attempt to appraise the overall effect of these variations on total costs and quality of output. We had hoped to be able to identify one or more instructional modes which would *both* lower costs and raise instructional quality when compared with the conventional plan. The programmed independent study plan is the clear winner on these counts, followed in order by the Ruml plan and possibly the Kieffer plan (depending upon the character of hardware and software systems adopted).

3. Methods of Calculating Costs

Before we can cost-out alternative modes of instruction, we will have to assemble some technical information and to develop some accounting techniques for the task. These are important matters of detail which most students of higher education's spiraling costs will wish to ponder before reviewing the results of our study, commencing in Chapter 4. Among them, for example, are our assumptions about the "production" characteristics of key instructional inputs, our methods of determining average unit "prices" of instructional inputs, and our "standard curriculum," i.e., the particular profile of disciplines and courses which anchors the study and makes possible meaningful cost comparisons between teaching methods.

FACULTY WORK LOADS If professional labor is the primary input into higher education's processes of production, then learning how faculty members spend their professional time ought to help us calculate the costs of alternative instructional modes. We especially need to know how much time full-time college teachers have available during a week or a semester for instructional purposes, e.g., to meet classes, seminars and tutorials; prepare for lectures and discussions; write, administer and grade examinations; design, supervise, and evaluate class projects; consult with students about instructional materials, etc., and we need to know as precisely as possible how the demands on instructional time of various instructional modes differ one from the other.

The full-time faculty member at a better-than-average small liberal arts college is responsible to many more constituencies than his students. As a professional person and member of a society of scholars, he needs and wants to keep constantly at the forefront of knowledge. Thus a faculty member sees research, writing, and creative acts as essential parts of his work life. As a member of a collegiate community, moreover, he is likely to share with his colleagues the administrative governance of the institution, at least by serving on one or more committees of his department or college and by participating in faculty meetings and collegiate forums. A faculty member may also be called upon to assume leadership in professional organizations or to advise community agencies. His experience in all these activities usually redounds to the students' benefit by broadening and deepening the faculty member's understanding of the worlds of scholarship and community life. Involved instructors usually make the best teachers.

A factual profile of workweek activities is only now beginning to emerge from so-called "faculty effort and output studies" at a few universities. Since no such studies seem to have been undertaken by smaller colleges, the authors enlisted the cooperation of their colleagues in the five undergraduate schools of the Claremont Colleges to develop one. Table 3 summarizes the results of our survey, which constructed a "typical" workweek during the 16-week spring semester, 1969–70. Approximately 60 percent of the nearly 400 full-time undergraduate faculty members in Claremont participated in the study.

The study found that the average workweek of a Claremont undergraduate faculty member during the academic year is about 55 hours and varies rather little between broad groups of disciplines. By far the largest chunk of his time is taken up by instruction, defined broadly to include preparations, seeing students in

TABLE 3
Allocation of average workweek, Claremont Colleges faculties* (in numbers of hours)

Disciplines	Average workweek	Average hours for instruction	Average hours in research activities
Natural sciences	56.9	37.9	11.2
Mathematics and engineering	53.8	34.0	11.3
Social sciences	54.6	33.7	13.2
Language and literature	52.1	39.0	8.2
Fine arts	54.5	33.3	15.4
Other humanities	56.9	40.6	9.2
All disciplines	54.8	36.4	11.4

*Excluding full-time graduate faculty.

class and out, and evaluating their work. Two-thirds of the time is so classified, though the proportion ranges widely among disciplines. If seeing students other than those registered with him in courses or for independent study is excluded from the instruction column, the average faculty member spends 33 hours per week in activities directly related to instruction (divided, roughly, between 27 hours for class-related activities and 6 hours for activities related to student independent study). He spends 11 more hours in scholarly, creative, and research activities, 5 more in department- or college-related administrative duties, and still 2 more in public service activities broadly related to his affiliation with the colleges at Claremont.

This portrait of a workweek differs somewhat from that painted by a faculty effort and output study conducted at the University of California. Its results are compared with Claremont's in Table 4. The major difference between the two sets of institutions, clearly, is the number of hours devoted to "research." Note, also, the much lower proportion of worktime devoted to instruction in the university system compared to the small colleges of Claremont.

There is a remarkable point of consistency among these and other studies which deserves special attention: Virtually all such studies reveal that the average college- and university-level teacher devotes between 30 and 35 hours per week to instructional activities. Other activities require varying amounts of time from school to school, but instruction seems remarkably constant. With some confidence, therefore, we have assumed in what follows that a

Average hours in administrative activities	Average hours of public service	Percent of workweek for instruction
7.0	0.8	66.6%
4.5	4.0	63.2
6.4	1.3	61.7
4.2	0.7	74.9
4.5	1.3	61.1
5.4	1.7	71.4
5.3	1.6	66.4

	Undergraduate faculties, Claremont Colleges	All faculties, University of California
Average workweek	55	60
Average hours for instruction	33*	30
Average hours in research activities	12	19
Average hours in adminis- trative activities	5	7
Average hours in other activities	5*	4
Percent of workweek directly related to instruction	60%	50%

TABLE 4
Allocation of average workweek, college versus university faculties (in number of hours)

*Adjusted to make definitions comparable with University of California data. "Other activities" include faculty involvement in "student affairs" as well as "public service."

SOURCE: University of California, Jan. 15, 1970.

"full-time teaching load," regardless of mode of instruction, is one which should absorb approximately 30 hours per week per instructor. (We have selected the lower edge of the range to pamper our hunch that most teachers gave themselves the benefit of the doubt in assigning numbers to the empty boxes of our questionnaire.) A semester's work load of teaching, then—spanning 15 weeks of classes and 1 week of examinations—should involve about 480 hours.

Table 5 tabulates for a hypothetical upper-division course in one of the social sciences how an instructor's time might be spent under the conventional, programmed independent study, Bakan, and Kieffer plans of instruction. In each case the number of students has been held to 20 to permit comparison between plans. One striking difference between plans is revealed in the column totals: For the same number of students, teaching modes differ widely in their time demands on instructors. A commitment under the conventional plan to spend 190 hours per semester on each course works out to a teaching load of 2½ courses per semester (480 hours of instruction divided by 190 hours per course), or 5 courses per year. The Bakan and Kieffer plans limit loads to 2 courses per semester, while the programmed independent study plan permits each instructor to teach 3½ courses per term.

TABLE 5 *Estimated time of instructor for alternative modes of instruction, upper-division social science course of 20 students (in number of hours per semester)*

Activity	Conven-tional	Programmed independent study	Bakan	Kieffer
Classroom:				
Lecture	25	4	15	3
Drill or discussion	20	8	15	
Seminar				22
Laboratory supervision				
Examination	4	3		10
Tutorials:				
Individual			120*	
Group				
Occasional interviews with students	15	30		30
Field work leadership				
Reading papers and exams	30	40	40	40
Preparation for course	90	40	40	100†
Clerical work	6	5	10	10
Supervision of learning station				‡
TOTAL HOURS PER SEMESTER	190	130	240	215

*Assumes six hours of tutorials for each student.
†Includes in Kieffer Plan pro-rata share of program preparation and updating.
‡Assumes for Kieffer Plan that learning stations can be supervised by technical assistants.

The reasons that the number of hours of instructional time differs between plans also are summarized in Table 5. Hours spent in the classroom, with students individually, and in various preparatory and evaluative activities, differ widely. The conventional plan is the most costly and the programmed independent study plan is the least costly in terms of classroom hours; the Bakan plan is made especially time-consuming for the instructor because of tutorials; and the conventional and Kieffer plans require relatively much time for course preparations.

Classroom activities, course preparations, and clerical work are relatively insensitive to changes in class enrollment for all these plans. For some of the plans, therefore, boosts in student enrollments per course may yield substantial savings for a college without overburdening instructors. This seems especially appropriate action for courses emphasizing relative independence of study, such as those taught in the programmed independent study and Kieffer plan styles, since little should be lost educationally by the change and only minor increases in interviewing and grading time need be absorbed by instructors. Raising student enrollments for Bakan plan courses, however, would be self-defeating because of the unusual demands of tutorials on instructors' time.

RANK DISTRIBUTION OF FACULTY
The price a college pays for its average instructor depends both upon the market-set level of compensation each segment (rank) of a faculty commands and upon the proportional share each seg-

TABLE 6
Average compensation and distribution of faculty by rank, selected liberal arts colleges, 1969–70

Institution	Average compensation, full-time faculty	Number professors	Number associate professors
A	$15,651	64	74
B	15,452	54	22
C	15,376	37	31
D	15,038	38	41
E	14,634	42	38
F	14,595	39	22
G	14,465	21	28
H	14,112	11	10
J	14,095	20	16
K	14,003	37	22
L	13,984	53	40
M	13,927	29	38
N	13,862	20	14
O	13,819	31	15
P	12,921	13	14
Q	12,617	17	16
R	12,255	25	6
S	11,609	15	24
T	11,381	13	14
TOTAL		596	504
Weighted average	$14,110		
Percent distribution of faculty by rank		28	24

SOURCE: AAUP *Bulletin,* June 1970.

ment of the faculty holds of the total. A faculty composed mostly of men and women in the lower ranks, other things equal, will be paid less per member than one consisting primarily of professors and associate professors. Some sense of how full-time faculties of small independent liberal arts colleges are distributed among academic ranks, therefore, is essential to our calculations of the costs of alternative modes of instruction.

Information about the rank distribution of faculties in 20 institutions, chosen to be representative of better quality liberal arts colleges nationally, is the subject of Table 6. It shows that full professors make up 28 percent of the sample, associate professors 24

Number assistant professors	Number instructors	Full-time faculty
70	11	219
58	3	137
45	37	150
61	13	153
47	21	148
37	20	118
21	12	82
19	3	43
21	12	69
31	29	119
37	29	159
50	28	145
20	11	65
24	9	79
28	12	67
28	24	85
11	8	50
18	7	64
21	5	53
687	336	2,145

32	16

percent, assistant professors 32 percent, and instructors 16 percent. Accordingly, slightly more than half of full-time faculty members are in ranks commanding relatively high levels of compensation (salaries and fringe benefits combined). This fact clearly helped to pull the average level of compensation above the $14,000 level in 1969–70.

FACULTY AND STAFF COSTS For ease of computation, the authors have rounded off the figure for average faculty compensation, found at the bottom of Table 6, to exactly $14,000. This amount, we have assumed, constitutes the price our hypothetical liberal arts college would have to pay per faculty member to obtain the services of a fully qualified professional staff. It includes gross salary to be charged to the instructional budget for a nine-month school year and all fringe benefits paid in cash or in kind by the college, such as the college's contributions to retirement funds, medical and life insurance premiums, faculty housing, etc. We also have assumed away any potential differences in average compensation between the disciplines.

Next, we have assumed that faculty members are entitled to a sabbatical leave of one semester at full pay each seventh year, and that the college has a generous policy on sick leave and termination of salary upon death. The experience of a number of colleges with which the authors are familiar suggests that these assumptions would raise faculty costs of instruction approximately 6 percent per year. The average faculty member's compensation of $14,000 per year then would become $14,840 for the purposes of calculating costs per course and per student.

On a per course basis, faculty costs would be $14,840, divided by the number of courses taught by an average instructor during the year. Unless it became necessary to pay teachers more to assure the success of particular courses, as under the Ruml plan for example, this method of calculating costs of faculty per course should work for any mode of instruction. Table 7 makes the calculation for various annual teaching loads.

Another related cost would be incurred when teaching assistants are hired to assist instructors with grading, preparing demonstrations, supervising laboratories, proctoring examinations, leading discussion sessions, and the like. In our calculations of costs per course, we have assumed that graduate assistants, faculty wives, and others serving as teaching assistants would be paid a full-time equivalent compensation of $6,500 for two semesters' work, includ-

TABLE 7
Faculty costs
per course

Annual course load	Faculty cost per course
2	$7,420
3	4,947
4	3,710
5	2,986
6	2,473
7	2,120

ing tuition remissions and other fringe benefits. Undergraduate students employed as assistants, on the other hand, would be paid at the rate of $2 per hour or $2,600 for nine months. Their costs on a per course basis are calculated in Table 8, assuming full-time employment. Costs on a half or quarter-time basis can be gotten by dividing the right-hand columns by 2 or 4, respectively.

Yet another related expense would be for secretarial and technical assistance within departments. We have assumed that a full-time secretary would be provided each seven faculty members at a total compensation of $4,500 per year. Thus, a five course per year teaching load per faculty member would allocate one-thirty-fifth of the secretary's compensation to each course, with appropriate changes in the fraction as teaching loads changed. Some science departments also would require stockroom clerks, shop technicians, electronic repairmen, etc., to man specialized facilities. We have assumed that four such persons would be sufficient to service the instructional programs of science departments, at an annual compensation per person of $8,000. The sum of $32,000 should be absorbed equally by the annual offering of laboratory science courses.

TABLE 8
Assistants'
costs per
course

Annual course load of instructor	Graduate assistant cost per course	Undergraduate assistant cost per course
2	$3,250	$1,300
3	2,167	867
4	1,625	650
5	1,300	520
6	1,083	433
7	929	371

COSTS OF PHYSICAL PLANT AND EQUIPMENT

Direct instructional costs would include not only staffing costs but a variety of additional outlays for offices and classrooms, equipment, instructional materials and supplies, library and computer services, and other instructional paraphernalia. The purpose of this section is to explain our methods of arriving at estimates of the per course costs of long-lived buildings and equipment.

Rather than trying to estimate the total investment in physical plant which would be needed to house the instructional activities of our hypothetical college of 1,200 students, and then amortizing it over the expected life of the buildings, we have chosen to follow a more direct route—that of estimating annual rental values for the space needed by alternative modes of instruction. The estimating procedure consists of (1) telling reputable leasing agents for commercial, industrial, and academic properties the size and nature of facilities desired and (2) obtaining from them approximate costs on a rental basis.

Whatever the instructional mode under consideration, each instructor would require an *office* which we have assumed would be assigned to him exclusively. If he is a scientist in need not only of office space to prepare lectures, answer mail, and consult students, but of dedicated research space as well, he probably would need more space than, say, his colleagues in the fine arts who would need practice as well as office space, and the latter, in turn, apparently would require more space than most of their colleagues in the social sciences and humanities. Specialization in office and research space needs, moreover, would create different rental rates per square foot of floor space fully furnished. To determine more exactly the nature of these differences we turned to the published standards of campus planners and architects as well as to the testimony of leasing agents. The results of our investigation are contained in the following calculations:

	Average space needed	Annual rental per sq ft	Annual cost per instructor
Office and research space for scientists	350 sq ft	$4.25	$1,488
Office and practice areas for artists and musicians	250 sq ft	4.00	1,000
Office space for others	150 sq ft	3.50	525

Annual course load	Office cost per course		
	Science	*Fine arts*	*Other*
2	$744	$500	$263
3	469	333	175
4	372	250	131
5	298	200	105
6	248	167	88
7	213	143	75

TABLE 9
Faculty office costs per course

Table 9 summarizes the costs per course of providing each instructor with a private office. It shows that office costs would vary in the same ways that staffing costs vary, i.e., according to the number of classes included in the teaching loads of instructors. The same table may be used to determine the costs of office space for full-time teaching assistants (or their equivalent); assuming that each office would be occupied by two persons rather than a single instructor, the numbers in Table 9 need only be divided by 2.

Classrooms, laboratories, and studios, however, would constitute the major share of facility needs for most instructional programs. Their costs per course would depend upon three variables: the average size of each specialized facility needed, the average rental value of each facility per square foot of floor space (adjusted to include related costs of corridors, lavatories, etc.), and the number of courses per year which could be scheduled per facility assuming realistic standards of occupancy. Perhaps an illustration would help. Suppose, initially, that courses would average 20 students per class. With the help of appropriate space standards, this would tell us how large the *average* room should be for each use. When multiplied by reasonable rental figures, the cost per annum of each facility could be obtained, as in the accompanying profile of space costs:

	Space needed	*Annual rental per sq ft*	*Annual cost per facility*
Science classroom	400 sq ft	$4.50	$1,800
Fine arts classroom	400 sq ft	4.25	1,700
Other classrooms	400 sq ft	3.50	1,400
Science laboratory	1,200 sq ft	4.50	5,400
Fine arts studio	900 sq ft	4.25	3,825

The assumptions made in this study about classroom occupancy rates differ according to type of facility. The average classroom for lecture-discussion courses in the social sciences and humanities, for example, has been scheduled to be used about 5 hours per day for 5 days a week, or a total of 25 hours per week. If each course using the room were to meet three times per week on the average, the room's rental cost should be shared by 8 courses per week (per semester), or 16 courses per year. A fall in the average number of meetings held by each course per week would have the effect of raising the room's capacity to serve many courses and of lowering the share of annual rental costs charged to each course. Classrooms for science and fine arts courses, on the other hand, because they are more specialized than other space, are assumed to be used only 18 hours per week. Rental charges should be appropriately higher per course. Then, too, most colleges schedule studio and laboratory sections only in the afternoons in order to minimize conflicts with other parts of the curriculum. This policy would effectively limit their average usage to 15 hours per week. Thus under the conventional plan, perhaps only 3½ laboratory science sections per semester could be accommodated in a given laboratory, forcing 7 courses (3½ per semester) to share the laboratory's (much higher) total rental, whereas 14 science courses could support a (lower-priced) science classroom. Other possibilities, differing according to the average number of hours per week each course would use each facility, are summarized in Table 10.

TABLE 10 Classroom, laboratory, and studio costs per course	Number of courses served per year	Cost per course, in thousands of dollars				
		Science classroom	Fine arts classroom	Other classrooms	Science laboratory	Fine arts studio
	6				900	638
	7				771	546
	8				675	478
	9				600	425
	10	180	170	140	540	383
	12	150	142	117		
	14	129	121	100		
	16	113	106	88		
	18	100	94	78		
	20	90	85	70		

Specialized equipment is used in many offices, classrooms, laboratories, and studios, along with standard furnishings and fixtures. For the most part, the annual rental fees used above take account of these needs. A few needs have been ignored in the calculations, however, and should be noted here. One such need would be special experimental equipment for science instructors' personal and exclusive use. To account for this, we have estimated that $400 should be added to the annual rental of each science instructor's office and that a smaller amount of $150 should be added for similar purposes to the office costs of fine arts instructors. These amounts, like the office rentals, should be spread across the number of courses taught per year by each instructor (see Table 9).

Another need would be the specialized audio-visual equipment required to implement remote controlled learning stations, such as found in the Kieffer plan. This equipment, at least in the systems design favored by Mr. Kieffer, is still in its technological infancy, and therefore is very hard indeed to cost-out with any reasonable degree of accuracy.

The system which best accords with the spirit of Kieffer's plan, to the best of our knowledge, is available from only one manufacturer. It is produced by Valtec Corporation of Irvine, California. The core of this system is a small computer dedicated entirely to the control of information flowing between input sources (a materials data bank) and output users (students at learning stations). It may, but need not, have access to larger computer installations on a campus. On the input side, it is linked with the data bank, which consists of any number of taped programs, each with its own audio-visual playback equipment and necessary relay connections. On the output side, the computer connects either directly through couplers to all learning stations or indirectly through several decentralized switching terminals to family clusters of learning stations. To obtain a particular lesson from the data bank, a student merely sits at a learning station carrel, punches the lesson's call numbers on a telephonelike keyboard, and waits briefly for the audio-visual response on his monitor and earphones.

This system has a number of important advantages over simpler, less costly, and probably less reliable ones. It stores all programmed materials in a central data bank rather than in decentralized cartridge or tape stations around the campus; this would reduce wear and tear on the tapes, limit the need for attendants, and make easier the withdrawal and introduction of old and new materials by instructors. The system also provides each student with the capacity to "control" programmed materials (starting, speeding up, reversing, and stopping at will) through the use of a simple keyboard without requiring him to handle the fragile tapes. And the system is modular, permitting additions of new input sources and learning stations a few at a time as the number of Kieffer plan classes expands and demand for programmed materials rises.

Its hardware costs would depend upon the character of Kieffer plan classes and the extent of their penetration into the curriculum. To simplify matters initially, let us assume the following: that 20 Kieffer plan classes per semester which depend heavily upon teaching-learning equipment would be offered; that each of these classes would have 60 rather than 20 student enrollments;[1] that each Kieffer plan class would have 5 "phases" of programmed materials, each containing 3 one-hour input sources or a total of 15 programmed hours per class; that each student would study programmed materials the equivalent of three times; that no class would extend beyond one semester in length; and that learning stations would remain open 100 hours per week while school was in session and that actual use would approximate 72 hours per week per station.

These assumptions permit us to estimate the size of the required hardware system. On the input side, 20 classes per semester, each with 15 one-hour input sources, would require 300 audio-visual playback units to house the programmed materials. On the output side, each learning station could accommodate 24 students per week using the station an average of 3 hours each; each 60-student class, therefore, would require the use of 2½ stations on a full-time basis, or 50 stations for the system as a whole. If classes were allowed to extend beyond the length of a semester, peak loading would dictate a higher capacity system of source units and learning stations.

A system of this design, if purchased outright, probably would cost in the neighborhood of $750,000. Our best estimate of the annual rental charge which would have to be made in order to amortize an equipment investment of this magnitude, maintain it, and house it properly is $140,000. Spread across 40 classes (20 each semester) and 2,400 student enrollments (40 classes times

---

[1] The reason for larger enrollments in Kieffer plan classes is efficiency, as shown in Chapter 4.

60 students per class), such a charge would amount to $3,525 per class or about $60 per student enrollment.

Approximately 80 percent of hardware costs for the Kieffer plan are associated with the input rather than output parts of the system. Changes in the number of students attending learning stations, therefore, would influence hardware costs considerably less than changes in the number of materials packages programmed in the data bank. Increasing the number of Kieffer plan classes or increasing the number of "phases" per class would almost certainly lead to large new investments in the system's hardware.

To illustrate these points, we have estimated that cutting the student enrollment of 40 Kieffer plan courses per year from 60 to 20 each would reduce hardware costs per course by only $300, or less than 10 percent of $3,525. By the same token, doubling the number of Kieffer plan courses (whatever the enrollment per course) or the number of hour-long source inputs per course would have no significant influence on hardware costs per course.

COURSE MATERIALS AND SUPPLIES Most courses, regardless of teaching method, require some outlays on duplicated materials, filmstrips, subscriptions, maps and charts, examination booklets, chalk, or other incidentals. In our calculations of instructional costs per course, we have estimated these outlays at $2 per student in lecture-discussion courses, $7.50 in fine arts courses, and $15 in laboratory science courses. Appropriate adjustments have been made for independent study courses and very large lecture courses.

Sometimes, too, courses require for their success an unusual amount of preparation time not only for the instructors but for assorted consultants and technicians as well. This is most likely to be the case with instructional modes like the Kieffer plan which would make use of custom-made programmed learning materials. Every mode of instruction, of course, requires instructors to spend time developing syllabi and series of prepared presentations, and most instructors, we gather, make use of some materials over and over again in successive years. In this sense, the "software" of every course may be regarded as a capital asset to be amortized over its useful life, just as we treated Kieffer plan software packages in the last chapter. But every class does not require outside technical assistance, nor do most classes require so much preparation time as those of the Kieffer plan. Even if the preparation time of Kieffer plan instructors were allocated directly to the individual time budgets of courses (and therefore were allowed to influence the size of teaching loads), as was done in Table 5, the remaining costs of producing software packages would need to be charged separately to the courses they were designed to serve.

The amount of outside preparation help which a Kieffer plan instructor would need is an open question. It might vary from a few days to several months of the time of a learning psychologist and an audio-visual technician, and from the purchase of commercially produced film sequences at relatively low prices to the costs of producing unique film sequences in campus studio facilities. To strike a happy medium, let us suppose in the beginning that the psychologist and technician each would spend two full weeks consulting with the instructor about course design and materials presentation. At the end of three years, the course would still be useful but would need "updating." The consultants would spend two more days apiece working with the instructor then. In three more years, the course would be judged obsolete and in need of total redesign. Thus, the life of the course would be six years, and the costs of software preparation and updating should be spread over the six times the course would be offered. (The costs of the instructor's time representing three months of full-time work to design the course and three additional weeks to update it, presumably would be taken into account in the assignment of teaching loads, according to Table 5.)

To provide the specialized consulting services required by the Kieffer plan, we assume that our college would retain a learning psychologist and an audio-visual specialist at prevailing average rates of faculty compensation, i.e., $14,840 each. Supporting office space, secretarial help, and other incidentals would bring the total of each up to $18,000 annually, making the total budget $36,000. The proportion of this amount which should be charged to a single course would be $2,250 for the initial consultation (2 weeks of work out of 32 working weeks), and $450 for the updating (2 days of work out of 160 working days). Since only one initial consultation and one updating occur during the six-year life of each course, these costs should be spread evenly across the six times the course would be offered. Thus the cost per course of technical assistance, under these assumptions, would approximate $450. The pro-rata share of purchased commercial film sequences probably would raise this figure to a total of $700 per course.

Library resources and services are an essential part of any instructional process. They are used by students enrolled in virtually all subject fields and courses, both as sources of independent study and research and as repositories of assigned or recommended reading materials. Faculty members, too, use them for course preparations, scholarly research, and browsing, as do visiting scholars, nonprofessional staff members, and townspeople.

For the purposes of this study, we have found it desirable to assume that the stock of books and level of library services are adequate, at some standard such as the Clapp-Jordan formula,[2] for the conventional plan of instruction. The annual direct costs to maintain such a library, then, would be its operating expenses and book acquisitions budgets. To this should be added an amount representing the implicit rental value of necessary space and equipment. Our calculations of these two kinds of expense are rough and ready indeed: direct operating expenses, we estimate, for a college of 1,200 students and 100 faculty members should be in the neighborhood of $170,000, and occupancy costs should approximate $130,000. The former figure, which was derived by formula, accords roughly with the average operating expenses reported by our panel of liberal arts colleges; the latter figure assumes 30,000 usable square feet of library space.

Since library facilities and services would be used by all fields and courses, we have assumed that their costs should be shared proportionally by courses according to enrollment. In the simplest possible curriculum model reviewed in the following section, the basic course of study would include 238 classes per semester, each with an enrollment of 20 students. In that conventional world, the $300,000 of annual library costs should be allocated evenly to 476 classes (2 semesters of 238 classes each), rendering a cost per class of $630.

Different modes of instruction would place different demands on library resources and services, however, making it necessary to devise ways of charging the costs of additional library services to particular plans. For modes of instruction emphasizing independent study, the Clapp-Jordan formula suggests that 12 additional volumes be added to conventional holdings for each full-time equivalent student in an honors or independent study program.

[2] See Clapp & Jordan, 1965, pp. 371–380.

If each additional volume costs $10.00 on the average, the total investment per student would be $16.30, assuming the books are treated as a capital outlay to be amortized over ten years at 6 percent interest. Staffing costs, according to another formula, would rise at the rate of approximately $14,000 annually for each 500 new full-time equivalent student users. Thus for each such student, annual staffing costs would rise $28.00. Together, annual outlays would rise $44.30 per student. If each student took eight courses emphasizing independent study during the year—a class load equivalent to a "full-time equivalent" student's work—the charge per student *per course* would be $5.54, and the additional amount allocable to each course would be $5.54 times the number of students enrolled in it.

The availability of high-capacity, versatile *computer* facilities and related "software" services is rapidly becoming as central to instructional processes as library resources. Unlike library services, however, computer services are used primarily by science students, sparingly by social science students, and hardly at all by students in the humanities. This means that the costs of maintaining an adequate set of computer services should be distributed *un*evenly among courses according to their expected demands on the facilities.

"Adequacy" is even harder to establish for computer services than for libraries, we have found. For want of a better standard, we have taken as a basis for our calculations the recommendations of the President's Science Advisory Committee in *Computers in Higher Education* (1967). Its report assumes that for most colleges it would be more efficient to participate with a large computing center (via remote consoles) on a time-shared basis than to maintain their own computing facilities. On this basis, the annual costs for a college of 1,200 students of operating a center, renting consoles and transmission lines, and providing appropriate programming and other software services was found to be approximately $150,000. This would be the cost exclusive of other noninstructional uses of the computer.

The experience of several collegiate computer centers with which we are familiar indicates that the students and staff of science courses, including courses in mathematics, account today for about 75 percent of console use. Another 20 percent is taken up by users in the social sciences, especially economics, and 5 percent of the time is used by humanists. Clearly, the diffusion of understanding about the operation and usefulness of computers is only beginning to take place outside of the sciences. On the basis of these estimates, $112,500 of the total cost of computer services should be spread across the number of science courses offered during the year, $30,000 should be charged to the annual social science offering, and $7,500 should be divided among the humanities offerings. The number of courses in each category of the conventional plan is given in the next section.

To the best of our knowledge, the computer sciences literature contains no standards, similar to the Clapp-Jordan formula for libraries, suggesting how experiments with independent study might influence computer usage. Our hunch is that it would accelerate interest among social scientists and humanists about computers as tools of research, and perhaps increase interest across the board. In the absence of solid evidence, however, we have chosen to make no adjustments of computer costs to reflect these possibilities.

THE CURRICULUM
Our hypothetical college has a curriculum similar to that of our sample of colleges, with these notable exceptions: First, the number of disciplinary fields (or clusters of fields) in which courses are offered has been limited to those which virtually every college offers; and second, the number of courses offered per semester within each field has been limited initially to a level somewhat below the common experience of better-than-average liberal arts colleges.

The effect of the first limitation can be seen in Table 11. It lists in descending order of frequency the titles of majors offered by one or another of the 20 colleges whose curricula we have studied in detail. The first 18 fields (marked with an *), because they are offered almost universally, constitute the "core" curriculum of our composite institution. For flexibility, a nineteenth undesignated field has been added to accommodate special interests, e.g., regional studies, or special requirements, e.g., education, which a particular college might feel obligated to include.

The effect of the second limitation can best be seen in Table 12. This table summarizes the judgments of seasoned teachers about the number of distinctly different courses (regardless of size) which should be offered annually within each discipline to service the needs of the whole college as well as to permit a major. In the views of our consultants, the figures appearing in the "low-prolif-

TABLE 11
Fields of concentration, selected liberal arts colleges

Field of concentration	Percent of colleges offering field
*Biology/Zoology	100
*Chemistry	100
*Economics	100
*English	100
*French	100
*History	100
*Mathematics	100
*Philosophy	100
* Political science	100
*Psychology	100
*Art	94
*Classics	94
*Physics and astronomy	94
*Religion	94
*Spanish	94
*German	88
*Music	88
*Sociology	88
Theatre arts	71
Education	59
Geology	59
Communications/Speech	53
Russian	53
Business administration	47
Regional studies	47
Anthropology	41
International relations	18
Botany	12
Geography	12
Urban studies	12
Dance	6
Ethnic studies	6

* SOURCE: Review of individual college catalogs.

eration" column represent the lowest possible numbers of courses which would meet these criteria. Two hundred twenty-five differ-ent courses limit choice severely, but a college wishing to prune

TABLE 12
"Standard"
curriculum
(in numbers of
courses per
year)

Disciplines	Degrees of course proliferation		
	Low	Moderate	High
Science:			
Biology	9	14	18
Chemistry	10	13	20
Physics	10	16	20
Social science:			
Economics	10	16	22
Political science	12	18	25
Psychology	10	16	22
Sociology	12	18	25
Language and literature:			
Classics	14	18	23
English	17	26	34
French	8	12	16
German	8	12	16
Spanish	8	12	16
Fine arts:			
Art	15	22	30
Music	15	22	30
Other disciplines:			
History	16	24	32
Mathematics	16	21	26
Philosophy	12	18	25
Religion	9	12	16
Other fields	14	25	34
Total number of courses	225	335	450

its curriculum back to this number, apparently, would not need to fear that by doing so it necessarily would do violence to agreed-upon professional standards. The "high-proliferation" column, on the other hand, summarizes what most department chairmen would like to have as a course offering, assuming few constraints on the availability of staff and other resources. Choice clearly is broadened by moving from left to right in Table 12—choice both for the student with specialized tastes and for the instructor eager to test out his newest fields of special interest on students. A surprisingly large number of the colleges in our sample conform to the high-proliferation model. The experience of a clear majority places them nearer it than to the low-proliferation column of the table.

The standard curriculum we have chosen takes the middle ground, identified in Table 12 as the moderate-proliferation model. It would call for 335 courses per year, or 167 per semester. Table 13 breaks down the semester figure into lower-division courses (primarily survey, principles, and tool courses) and upper-division offerings (more specialized and advanced courses rarely available to freshmen). Again, the figures are based on the judgments of academic consultants experienced in teaching at colleges of the

TABLE 13
Distribution of courses by field, "moderate-proliferation" model, "typical semester"

	Lower division	*Upper division*	*Total*
Science:			
Biology	1	6	7
Chemistry	1½	5	6½
Physics	3	5	8
Social science:			
Economics	2½	5½	8
Political science	3	6	9
Psychology	1	7	8
Sociology	2	7	9
Language and literature:			
Classics	3	6	9
English	4½	8½	13
French	3	3	6
German	3	3	6
Spanish	3	3	6
Fine arts:			
Art	4	7	11
Music	2	9	11
Other:			
History	3	9	12
Mathematics	4	6½	10½
Philosophy	2	7	9
Religion	2	4	6
Other	4	8½	12½
Total number of courses per semester	51½	116	167½

sort which concern us. Note especially that more than two-thirds of all courses are classified as upper-division.

In most small liberal arts colleges, courses with large potential enrollments are sectioned into several smaller classes in order to preserve the possibility of close faculty-student contact. The number of classes which must be staffed, therefore, normally is higher than the number of course offerings. To get from the one to the other we need to know how student enrollments typically are distributed among fields and types of courses. Table 14 provides

TABLE 14 *Distribution of student enrollments, hypothetical college of 1,200 students, "typical semester"*

	Lower division	Upper division	Total	Percent distribution of total
Science:				
Biology	135	200	335	7.0
Chemistry	125	115	240	5.0
Physics	115	65	180	3.8
Social science:				
Economics	125	90	215	4.5
Political science	140	155	295	6.1
Psychology	75	215	290	6.0
Sociology	140	160	300	6.1
Language and literature:				
Classics	20	55	75	1.6
English	215	380	595	12.4
French	130	65	195	4.1
German	105	25	130	2.7
Spanish	60	40	100	2.1
Fine arts:				
Art	160	95	255	5.3
Music	105	45	150	3.1
Other:				
History	135	220	355	7.4
Mathematics	205	130	335	7.0
Philosophy	100	135	235	4.9
Religion	140	80	220	4.6
Other	145	155	300	6.3
Total student enrollments per semester	2,375	2,425	4,800	100.0

this information. It is constructed on the assumptions that all courses are "full" courses, i.e., that they carry four credits, and that students normally would take four courses each semester. Thus, there would be 4,800 enrollments each semester, or 9,600 enrollments each year. The distribution of enrollments in a typical semester among fields and between lower and upper division, revealed in Table 14, is based on our analysis of actual enrollment patterns in 12 of the 20 colleges in our sample.

With one further assumption, namely, that all large courses would be sectioned into classes of no more than 30 students each, Table 14 permits us to calculate the number of classes which would have to be offered in order to teach our standard curriculum in a

TABLE 15
Distribution of classes by field, "moderate proliferation" model, "typical semester"

	Lower division	Upper division	Total
Science:			
Biology	5	9	14
Chemistry	4½	6	10½
Physics	4	6	10
Social science:			
Economics	4½	6	10½
Political science	5	7	12
Psychology	3	8	11
Sociology	5	7	12
Language and literature:			
Classics	3	6	9
English	9	16	25
French	5	4	9
German	4	4	8
Spanish	3	4	7
Fine arts:			
Art	7	7	14
Music	4	9	13
Other:			
History	5	12	17
Mathematics	8	8	16
Philosophy	4	8	12
Religion	5	5	10
Other	6	12	18
Total number of classes per semester	94	144	238

conventional way. Table 15 shows the results. It suggests that a moderately proliferated curriculum with sectioning of large courses would require our hypothetical college to schedule 238 classes per semester. It implies, moreover, that these classes, since they are to serve 4,800 student enrollments, would contain 20 students each on the average.

In the next chapter we shall want to work with as few categories of classes as possible in order to simplify the process of costing-out several modes of instruction. Table 15 is needlessly detailed for that purpose. The following summary, which groups classes according to their potential degree of costliness, should suffice:

	Per semester	Per year
Science classes with laboratory	22	44
Other science classes	12	24
Fine arts classes with studio	12	24
Other fine arts classes	15	30
Language classes with laboratory	14	28
Social science classes	45½	91
Other classes (mostly humanities)	117½	235
TOTAL CLASSES	238	476

4. *The Costs of Instruction*

This chapter contains our estimates of the relative costliness of alternative modes of instruction. It begins with the conventional plan, the traditional and strikingly durable mode of instruction which dominates liberal education in this country. We test the sensitivity of its costs per course and per student to changes in faculty teaching loads, numbers of classes, total enrollments, the distribution of faculty ranks, and the disciplinary mix of classes. Each, we find, influences the costs of instruction in significant ways, and together, they alone could provide an abundant harvest of savings if manipulated in appropriate ways. We then go on to identify the costs and latent economies (if any) of the Ruml plan, the programmed independent study plan, a variant of the Bakan plan, and the Kieffer plan.

The authors know only too well that the particular assumptions made here and in Chapter 3 have severely limited the number of comparisons between plans which could and indeed should be made. In as many cases as possible, we have tried to arm the reader with sufficient tools to make his own calculations of costs based on different assumptions. We hope that he will use them freely, and perhaps make them available to others.

CONVEN-TIONAL PLAN Our beginning point is familiar to most readers: College has just opened for the fall semester, its 1,200 students and 100 faculty members back from the activities of a summer. Registration and the opening convocation are over, and the routines of campus life have been established. Most students are enrolled in four classes of varied sizes, but the registrar's records show that the average class has exactly 20 student enrollments. Most lecture-discussion classes in the humanities and social sciences meet three times per week for 50 minutes, and most laboratory and studio courses meet twice a week for lectures and discussion and once or twice more, usually during a whole afternoon, for laboratory and studio practice. The science faculty averages teaching loads of two classes per semester per instructor, as does the faculty involved in the fine arts studio programs. Other faculty members teach two or three classes, averaging 2½ apiece. Twenty departments offer courses, and the class schedule indicates that 238 classes are being offered. All are taught in conventional ways.

Chapter 3, which describes in considerably greater detail the chief features of this college, makes it possible to ask just how much instruction would cost per course and per student in this arrangement of courses and teaching methods. Staff, facilities,

TABLE 16
Estimated cost per class and per student of conventional plan of instruction

	Laboratory science class	Other science class	Fine arts studio class
Staff:			
Instructor	$3,710	$3,710	$3,710
Assistants	217		
Secretarial	161	161	161
Technical	727		
Facilities:			
Instructor's office	372	372	250
Assistant's office	22		
Secretarial office	19	19	19
Classroom	100	150	71
Laboratory or studio	771		546
Other facilities	60		161
Equipment: Instructor's office	100	100	37
Supplies and materials	300	80	150
Total direct instructional costs per class	$6,559	$4,592	$5,105
Costs per student	$ 328	$ 230	$ 255
Library	$ 630	$ 630	$ 630
Computer	1,654	1,654	24
Total indirect instructional costs per class	$2,284	$2,284	$ 654
Costs per student	$ 114	$ 114	$ 33
Total direct and indirect instructional costs per class	$8,843	$6,875	$5,759
Cost per student	$ 442	$ 344	$ 288

equipment, supplies, library, and computer services would all contribute to instructional costs in different ways, depending upon the particular design of each course. For this reason, we have found it necessary to separate classes into seven different categories, each containing a group of courses with similar cost characteristics. The categories selected include: laboratory science classes, other science classes, studio classes in the fine arts, other fine arts classes, language classes requiring laboratory, other lecture-discussion classes in the humanities, and lecture-discussion classes in the social sciences.

Table 16, which assumes that *all* classes have enrollments of

| Other fine arts class | Language class | Other lecture-discussion | |
		Humanities class	Social science class
$2,986	$2,986	$2,986	$2,986
129	129	129	129
	286		
200	105	105	105
15	15	15	15
106	88	88	88
	161		
37			
40	40	40	40
$3,513	$3,810	$3,363	$3,363
$ 176	$ 191	$ 168	$ 168
$ 630	$ 630	$ 630	$ 630
24	24	24	330
$ 654	$ 654	$ 654	$ 960
$ 33	$ 33	$ 33	$ 48
$4,167	$4,464	$4,017	$4,323
$ 208	$ 223	$ 201	$ 216

20 students each, summarizes the principal elements of instructional cost for each of the seven categories of classes. For those who prefer to distinguish between direct and indirect instructional costs, the table is arranged with two subtotals making this distinction. Staffing costs, clearly, would make up most of the direct costs per course. Facility costs would bulk large only for laboratory and studio classes. And supplies and equipment (other than equipment normally provided with classroom and laboratory facilities) would seem insignificant. Indirect instructional costs, on the other hand, would be highly significant: had they been allocated equally among course categories—as, indeed, the library portion of indirect costs were allocated—library and computer services together would seem to have cost nearly $1,000 for each class taught during the year.

Table 16 indicates clearly that some classes would cost much more than others. As a result of lumping direct and indirect instructional costs together (as we shall do throughout the remainder of this chapter) and dividing by the number of students per class, the bottom line shows that laboratory science classes would be more than twice as expensive per student as lecture-discussion classes in either the humanities or social sciences. The reasons also are clear: Science instructors would teach fewer classes per year, making it necessary to charge a larger fraction of their compensation to each class than for other instructors; science classrooms and laboratories would cost more to provide and would be used less intensively than other facilities; laboratory science instruction would require substantial inputs of supervisory and technical assistance; and science instruction would lead to relatively heavy use of expensive computer facilities and services.

Effects of Teaching Load Changes

One potential source of greater efficiency and lower cost at liberal arts colleges is increased teaching loads. By raising the average number of courses offered by instructors each year, say, by one course, substantial savings ought to be recorded in the sections of Table 16 which are labeled "Staff" and "Facilities." The amount of a social science instructor's annual compensation charged in the right-hand column of the table, for example, would drop from $2,986 per class to $2,473 as his annual load rose from five to six classes. Similar but smaller changes also would be recorded in the per class compensation of assistants and secretarial help, and in the costs of providing staff offices. For a class in the social sciences, the overall effect of adding one class per year to each instructor's teaching schedule would be to reduce class costs from $4,323 to $3,769, and costs per student enrollment from $216 to $188. The effect of such a change on other categories of classes is summarized in columns 3 and 6 of Table 17.

Table 17 also shows the influence on costs of *reducing* teaching loads by one class per year. Note, in the latter case, that per student costs of offering a social science class would *rise* from $216 to $254. Since a lighter load is the direction toward which most faculty members would prefer to move, readers may wish to study columns 1 and 4 of Table 17 very carefully.

When faculty teaching loads change, so, too, should the size of the faculty change. If the number of classes offered by the college are held constant, an increase of teaching loads by one course per year should permit the college (through attrition over a number of years) to reduce the number of faculty members from 100 to 83. Similarly, a reduction of teaching loads by an equal amount probably would lead to faculty hiring—eventually to the level of 127 members.

At best, raising teaching loads would be politically difficult to arrange. Most faculties believe that teaching loads already are too high and should be reduced. But some faculty members might agree to increased loads if sufficient incentives to take on the burdens of an additional course were offered. Bribes, in short,

TABLE 17 *Effects of teaching load changes on estimated average cost per class, conventional plan**

	Average cost per class			Average cost per student		
Type of class	"Light" load	Standard load	"Heavy" load	"Light" load	Standard load	"Heavy" load
Laboratory science	$10,348	$8,843	$7,940	$517	$442	$397
Other science	8,302	6,876	6,022	415	344	301
Studio fine arts	7,151	5,759	4,942	358	288	247
Other fine arts	4,990	4,167	3,590	250	208	180
Language	5,250	4,464	3,910	262	223	195
Other humanities	4,803	4,017	3,457	240	201	173
Social science	5,085	4,323	3,769	254	216	188
Weighted average	5,702	4,789	4,170	285	240	208

* Standard load would be five classes per year for instructors of lecture-discussion courses, and four per year for science and studio fine arts instructors. A "light" load would consist of one less course per year than standard load, and a "heavy" load would mean one more course per year than the standard.

may succeed where appeals to loyalty and the reduction of mounting deficits might not.

To attract interest in higher teaching loads, suppose that each regular member of the faculty were offered the equivalent of a full-time (undergraduate) teaching assistant in return for his agreement to teach one more course per year. Table 18 summarizes the effects such an offer would have on class costs. Clearly, even as substantial an offer as this one would raise costs insufficiently to wipe out the potential savings of increased faculty teaching loads. Some saving still would remain after payment of the bribe. Alternatively, agreeable faculty could be offered the cash equivalent of a full-time assistant over and beyond his usual compensation, still leaving the college with a net saving. The latter arrangement would not produce the same desirable side effect as the first, however, in that it would not provide additional income to needy students. Nor would it be desirable, we hasten to add, if it resulted in shortened class preparations or fewer hours devoted to remaining at some professional research frontier.

Effects of Reducing the Number of Classes Offered Another potential source of cost savings is pruning the class schedule. We have, until now, assumed the correctness of the moderate-proliferation model which prescribes 335 courses (see Table 12) and 476 classes per year (see Table 15). Now we should

TABLE 18 *Effects of increased teaching assistance on estimated average cost per class, conventional plan*

Type of class	Average cost per class				
	Heavy load	Net additions for assistant*	Adjusted heavy load	Standard load	Net saving
Laboratory science	$7,940	$572	$8,512	$8,843	$331
Other science	6,022	572	6,594	6,876	282
Studio fine arts	4,942	572	5,514	5,759	245
Other fine arts	3,590	477	4,067	4,167	100
Language	3,910	477	4,387	4,464	77
Other humanities	3,457	477	3,934	4,017	83
Social science	3,769	477	4,246	4,323	77
Weighted average	4,170	502	4,672	4,789	117

* Net additions include the appropriate share of each assistant's $2,600 of total compensation and the costs of office space.

drop the assumption and explore the effects on costs of cutting the class schedule and raising the average size of classes. Since our academic consultants agree that a low-proliferation model is educationally feasible, let us consider its implications.

The low-proliferation model calls for 225 courses per year. Our analysis, which is similar to that employed in the development of Table 15, suggests that this number of courses would lead to no fewer than 320 classes, none any larger than 40 students. Thus, movement from the moderate- to low-proliferation model would create a potential of cutting classes by one-third and of raising their average size by one-half (from 20 to 30). Assuming a standard (2½ courses per semester) teaching load, implementation of the low-proliferation model also would imply a reduction in the number of faculty members from 100 to 67 (again, by attrition).

Costs per class would be substantially higher in the low- than in the moderate-proliferation model, primarily because very large (but slightly reduced) total outlays for library and computer services would have to be spread over fewer classes and because classroom, laboratory, and studio facilities would need to be enlarged to accommodate higher enrollments per class. Costs per student enrollment would be made considerably lower, however, due to the more than offsetting effects on average costs of higher student enrollments per class. Table 19 shows the difference.

TABLE 19 *Effects of reducing the number of classes offered on estimated average cost per class and per student, conventional plan*

Type of class	Number of classes per year		Average costs per class		Average cost per student	
	Moderate*	Low*	Moderate	Low	Moderate	Low
Laboratory science	44	32	$8,843	$10,350	$442	$345
Other science	24	16	6,876	7,620	344	254
Studio fine arts	24	16	5,759	6,159	288	205
Other fine arts	30	20	4,167	4,193	208	140
Language	28	20	4,464	4,682	223	156
Other humanities	235	148	4,017	4,034	201	134
Social science	91	68	4,323	4,438	216	148
	476	320				
Weighted average			$4,789	$5,087	$240	$170

* Degree of class proliferation.

Once again, the true potential of reductions in the number of classes would be governed by faculty attitudes toward such cuts. Most faculty members dislike increases in the size of their classes almost as much as they abhor heavier teaching loads. Indeed, both vehicles of cost saving would burden faculty members with more students than previously. An offer, similar to the one suggested in the previous section, might be made as a means to assent. In both instances, smaller bribes to obtain smaller concessions, e.g., teaching load increases of only one-half course per year or class cuts from 476 to only 400, would be entirely possible, of course.

Effects of Increasing the Number of Class Enrollments

A result similar to pruning the class schedule might be achieved by increasing the size of the student body while holding the number of classes constant. Consider the possible effects on average costs, for example, of increasing enrollments 50 percent, from 9,600 class registrations per year to 14,400. With 476 classes offered each year, average class size once again would reach the level of 30. These assumptions would yield a cost per student enrollment of $172, approximately the same as that for the low-proliferation model serving 1,200 students, and substantially below $240 (Table 17), the average cost per student enrollment for the moderate-proliferation model with a third fewer students. We shall say more about the potential economies of larger-sized student bodies in Chapter 6.

Effects of Changing the Distribution of Faculty Ranks

The proportion of faculty members in a given rank varies widely among colleges, according to Table 6. Our procedure in Chapter 3 was to hide these variations in an average distribution of faculty ranks for our 20-college sample. This distribution, the reader will recall, when applied to salary and fringe benefit information for each rank, yielded the figure for average faculty compensation of $14,000 used until now in this study. Now we should explore the effects on costs per student enrollment of allowing the rank distribution to vary, at least within the limits set by our 20-college sample.

These limits are described in the table of rank profiles (p. 57). Note that College L supports in the tenured ranks almost two-

	College L ("top-heavy" rank distribution),%	College X (average rank distribution),%	College U ("bottom-heavy" rank distribution),%
Professors	36	28	14
Associate professors	28	24	16
Assistant professors	21	32	34
Instructors	14	16	36

thirds of its faculty, whereas less than one-third of college U's faculty has achieved the ranks of associate professor or full professor.

When these extreme cases are applied to the compensation scale first used in our study—a scale which roughly accords with the midpoint between A and B ratings in the AAUP's average compensation scale for 1969–70—average compensation for all ranks would become $14,610 in the first instance and $11,750 in the second. A 6 percent upward adjustment for sabbaticals and death benefits would raise the figures to $15,490 and $12,460, respectively. Thus, there are substantial savings possible in staff costs by altering downward the average age and rank of a college faculty. A movement from the profile of College X to College U, for example, would reduce average costs per student enrollment from $240 to $214. A movement from College X to College L, on the other hand, would raise costs to $251.

Effects of Changing the Mix of Classes Offered

Some types of classes cost more than others. In general, laboratory science classes are the most costly, followed in order by other science classes, studio fine arts classes, language classes, social science classes, non-studio fine arts classes, and other humanities classes. Rearranging the distribution of classes offered in each category, therefore, ought to permit changes in overall costs per course and per student enrollment.

A 10 percent reduction in the number of classes offered in each of the first four categories, for example, accompanied by an offsetting increase in the number of courses offered in the last three, would leave the total number of classes unchanged but would reduce the average cost per course from $4,789 to $4,729, and the average cost per student enrollment from $240 to $236. Thus, incremental changes—as compared with structural ones—in the mix of classes offered would make relatively little difference to the cost of instruction collegewide.

THE RUML PLAN

The Ruml plan is yet another variation on the conventional plan, this time one in which cost is influenced by changes in the size distribution of classes. The Ruml plan does have another implication, however. It is a product of the general education movement, and it implies in its large lecture courses an emphasis on the integration of learning. Ruml plan courses would not be narrow disciplinary experiences, as conventional plan courses frequently are accused of being. Rather, they would range broadly over fields of knowledge, weaving information and insights into a single, integrated whole. In this sense, the Ruml plan is as much a proposal to reform curricular content as to change teaching method. We include it here as a unique mode of instruction and also as a serious statement of an educational philosophy.

The first step in costing-out the Ruml plan is to develop a profile of classes. It must include, of course, several large lecture courses. These, we assume, should accommodate 300 students each. The rest of the classes should be drawn from conventional disciplines, enough to permit each department the minimum number of courses specified in the low-proliferation model. None of these classes

TABLE 20
Ruml plan schedule of classes and enrollments per year

	Numbers of classes			
	Conventional plan	Ruml plan	Average enrollment	Total enrollment
Large science lectures		2	300	600
Large non-science lectures		6	300	1,800
Laboratory science	44	32	20	640
Other science	24	17	20	340
Studio fine arts	24	17	15	255
Other fine arts	30	22	15	330
Languages	28	28	25	700
Social sciences	91	72	22	1,585
Other	235	168	20	3,360
TOTAL	476	364		9,600

should exceed 30 students each, and together they should average about 20. Table 20 summarizes a class schedule which conforms to this set of assumptions and accords with our normal distribution of enrollments (see Table 14).

The next step is to establish the costs of a large lecture course. The instructor, we shall assume, would be paid $25,000 annually for his services, including all fringe benefits. He would be required to teach only one course per semester and would be furnished the services on a full-time basis of both an undergraduate and a graduate assistant. They, like he, would need an office, and an auditorium would have to be provided for the class meetings. Common reading materials in the library would need to be duplicated to accommodate such large course enrollments, but their standardization for a major share of the student body would reduce the number of different volumes needed appreciably, producing net savings in library services. Computer services, we have assumed, would be used on a per student basis approximately one-half of normal in large lecture courses.

Table 21 reflects these assumptions in the calculation of course costs for 300-student lecture courses in sciences and other fields. A large lecture course in general science would cost approximately $40,000 and one in the humanities or social sciences about $27,000. On a per student basis, including all direct and indirect instructional costs, the corresponding figures would be $133 and $89, respectively.

The latter figures pertain to approximately one quarter of all student enrollments. The other three quarters would be in conventional courses whose costs we may assume are the same as appeared in Tables 16 and 17. Put together, they would produce average costs per student enrollment of $202—a saving of $38 per student enrollment below the conventional plan.

THE PROGRAMMED INDEPENDENT STUDY PLAN This plan, too, may be linked to conventional plans. It was noted in Chapter 3 that a primary source of potential savings in this plan is in the number of courses faculty could offer. Because independent study would relieve instructors from some preparatory and classroom duties, they would need to budget fewer hours per course than for conventional plan arrangements (see Table 5). This fact would permit them to teach more classes per year, and it would allow their institutions to husband expensive resources. Thus, the effects on costs of introducing programmed independent study

	Large lecture	
	Science	*Non-science*
Staff:		
Instructor	$12,500	$12,500
Assistants	4,550	4,550
Secretary	565	565
Technical	150	
Facilities:		
Instructor's office	744	263
Assistant's office	263	263
Secretary's office	66	66
Classroom	2,000	2,000
Equipment:		
Instructor's office	200	
Other	100	
Supplies and materials:		
Supplies	3,000	600
Software	250	150
Library	5,000	5,000
Computer	10,500	705
TOTAL COST PER COURSE	$39,888	$26,662
COST PER STUDENT	$ 133	$ 89

would not be unlike those of teaching load changes which were outlined above.

Table 22 illustrates the costs which would be incurred if independent study classes were substituted for conventional ones in the most populous parts of the curriculum. The first two columns summarize the elements of cost in standard-sized classes in the social sciences and humanities. They are constructed on the assumption that each instructor would be able to teach seven rather than five classes per year as his normal load. This is an appropriate assumption, we believe, because each class would take only 130 hours of instructor time (according to Table 5), compared with 190 hours per class under the conventional plan. The column totals reflect this difference: on a cost per student enrollment basis, a programmed independent study social science class of 20 students would cost $173 as compared with $216 with conventional teaching methods; an independent study class in the humanities would cost $158 per student compared with $201 if conventionally taught. Conversion of one-half the normally scheduled lecture-discussion classes in these fields to independent study would lower the overall average cost per student enrollment from $240 to $225, a significant saving without altering the average size or number of classes.

The right-hand columns of Table 22 explore the dramatic effects on costs of altering the size of independent study classes. A careful analysis of faculty time budgets has convinced us that, with minor help from a part-time teaching assistant, each instructor could teach four independent study classes per year with enrollments of 60 rather than 20 students each. This would have the effect of raising the student load per faculty member from 140 to 240 per year, greatly boosting productivity. For the student, it would reduce the range of independent study options available, since it would cut the number of independent study classes by two-thirds (while holding the number of student enrollments in independent study constant). In cost terms, to increase the enrollment of each course would reduce the per student expense of independent study classes in the social sciences to $129 and in the humanities to $114. In combination with other conventional classes, the two kinds of instruction and class sizes would produce costs per student enrollment of $207. Another way of putting this is to say that the introduction of approximately 54 large (60-student) independent study classes, representing one-third of all student enrollments, would reduce costs per student about 15 percent (from $240 to $207).

THE BAKAN PLAN The Bakan plan departs sharply from conventional plans in several respects. Instead of specifying beforehand the fields and subjects to be offered, the plan would let individual instructors decide what to teach and how to teach it. Instead of expecting students to attend frequently scheduled classes for lecture and drill, the plan would insist that students meet *individually* with their instructors several times during the semester. Instead of forcing students into the lockstep of highly structured course outlines, the plan would encourage relative independence of study. And instead of scheduling a large number of classes each semester in order to broaden student choice and cater to the wishes of faculty, the Bakan plan would deliberately constrict the class schedule (and honor faculty wishes another way).

Since students and faculty would be free under the Bakan plan

		Social science class of 20 students	Humanities class of 20 students
Staff:			
	Instructor	$2,120	$2,120
	Assistant		
	Secretary	92	92
Facilities:			
	Instructor's office	75	75
	Assistant's office		
	Secretary's office	10	10
	Classroom	50	50
Supplies		40	40
Library:			
	Basic share	630	630
	Adjustment for independent study	111	111
Computer		330	24
TOTAL COST PER CLASS		$3,458	$3,152
COST PER STUDENT ENROLLMENT		$ 173	$ 158

TABLE 22
Estimated costs per class and per student, programmed independent study plan

to take and offer whatever courses they pleased, the proportion of classes offered in different fields might differ widely from that of the conventional plan. We have no way of predicting the choices which actually would be made; so we have assumed a class mix, though freely selected, identical with a conventional curriculum. Our reference point for constructing it is Table 19: having assumed a faculty of 100 and a faculty course load of 4 courses per year under the plan, we have chosen a class schedule midway between the low- and moderate-proliferation models:

	Number of classes per year
Laboratory science	38
Other science	20
Studio fine arts	20
Other fine arts	25
Languages	24
Social sciences	80
Other humanities	193
	400

Social science class of 60 students	*Humanities class of 60 students*
$3,710	$3,710
217	217
161	161
131	131
22	22
19	19
140	140
120	120
1,890	1,890
330	330
990	72
$7,730	$6,812
$ 129	$ 114

Faculty members also would be free under the Bakan plan to select whatever mode of instruction that best fits the subject matter at hand and their own repertoire of teaching skills. "The actual conduct of a course may be quite conventional," Professor Bakan has written, "or as unconventional as may appear appropriate." Again, we have difficulty predicting how various faculties would teach different subjects. One shred of evidence is our interview notes: The academic consultants *least* able to see how their existing modes of instruction could be changed were from the sciences and the studio fields of fine arts. The reason may be that these fields, more than any other, already are being taught as modified tutorials. Whatever the reason, we have assumed in the following calculations that all classes in non-studio fine arts, social sciences, and other humanistic studies are taught as tutorialized independent study, and that all other classes, including languages, sciences, and studio courses, are taught as they are at present.

The results of the calculations are summarized in Table 23. Costs per student enrollment for the three tutorialized fields would be $238, $247, and $232, respectively, compared with $208, $216, and $201 for the same fields taught conventionally. Combin-

TABLE 23 Estimated cost per class, Bakan plan		Fine arts classes (non-studio)
Staff:		
	Instructor	$3,710
	Secretary	161
Facilities:		
	Instructor's office	250
	Secretary's office	19
	Classroom	53
Supplies		42
Library:		
	Basic Share	630
	Adjustment for independent study	117
Computer		24
	TOTAL COST PER CLASS	$5,006
	COST PER STUDENT ENROLLMENT*	$ 238

*Average enrollment per class of 21.

ing these results with the information contained in Table 16 for other fields permits us to develop an overall estimate of Bakan plan costs. It suggests that the Bakan plan method of independent study—or more accurately, the version of the Bakan plan which our assumptions have caused us to explore—would cost approximately $261 per student enrollment, or $21 more per enrollment than our basic conventional plan.

Unlike the programmed independent study plan, this plan's costs would be very sensitive to changes in the average size of classes. Since the lion's share of instructors' time would be occupied with individual tutorials, faculty time commitments would rise almost proportionally with class size. Harvesting savings by boosting class sizes, therefore, would not be available. The one exception to this generalization lies with the Ruml plan. Were a few large lecture courses grafted onto the Bakan plan, the savings associated with their presence in the curriculum would help to finance deeper penetration of tutorials into otherwise standardized courses of study.

The major conclusion from our exploration of the Bakan plan is that tutorial instruction is possible within a reasonable budget

Social science classes	Other humanities classes
$3,710	$3,710
161	161
131	131
19	19
44	44
42	42
630	630
117	117
330	24
$5,184	$4,878
$ 247	$ 232

if an institution wishes to make the necessary adjustments. In the past, the tutorial method has tended to be dismissed without examination as beyond our means.

THE KIEFFER PLAN Of all the plans we have selected to investigate, the Kieffer plan is the most original and the least easy to make specific. It stands apart from other plans for its mode of preparation, its rearrangement of the college calendar, the freedoms it grants students, and its uses of modern learning equipment. Yet, by its designer's own admissions, major variations are possible in the software production process, the elaborateness of programmed materials, the expected life of prepared programs, the sophistication of learning equipment, the schedule of equipment operation, the uses of assistants, the number of programmed "phases," the frequency and length of seminars, the official duration of each course, the flexibility of examination times, the amount of written work, the extent of student conferences, and the schedule of plan adoption among a faculty's members.

Clearly, the range of possible Kieffer plan costs is enormous. At the one extreme, the Kieffer plan closely resembles the Bakan plan of tutorial study. If one thinks of the library as its battery of learning stations and of its seminars (for a small Bakan-sized class) as individual or group tutorials, one need only impose limits on the duration of the course to make it seem like a Bakan plan class. This model is probably the *least* costly form that a small Kieffer plan class might take in a college like the one of this study. At the opposite extreme, it is possible to imagine an equally small Kieffer plan class being offered after lengthy and expensive preparations, with extensive audio-visual communication, over an abbreviated useful life, whose costs would exceed those of any known mode of instruction. The challenge of this section is to find a middle position which does justice to Dr. Kieffer's intent and produces confidence in the comparisons drawn from it.

Work on such a position was begun in the last chapter. To prepare the programmed material, for example, we assumed that each Kieffer plan professor would spend an average of 16 weeks every 6 years designing and updating the program, and that he would be helped in the process by a learning psychologist and an audio-visual specialist working 12 days each on the project. At appro-

	20-student classes	
TABLE 24 *Estimated time costs per instructor, Kieffer plan, 20- and 60- student classes (in hours per class per semester)*	*Laboratory classes*	*Classes high on drill and practice*
Classroom:		
Lecture	3	3
Seminars	22	22
Laboratory supervision	30	
Examination	10	10
Student interviews	10	30
Reading papers and exams	50	40
Preparation for course	100	100
Clerical work	10	10
Learning station supervision	*	*
Total hours per class	235	210
Less hours delegated to assistants		30
Net hours	235	190
Faculty teaching load per year	4	5

* A computer-controlled local lesson control system requires no on-the-spot instructor supervision. Other systems might.

priate compensation rates, we determined that the specialists' time was worth approximately $2,700 and that other purchased materials (for use on learning station equipment) probably would add $1,500 to this amount. The sum, allocated evenly to the six times the course would be offered, yielded a cost per course for programmed materials (excluding the value of the instructor's time) of $700. For courses making use of the library as a learning station, this figure has been reduced to $450.

We also attempted in Chapter 3 to estimate the costs of modern learning equipment. The range of possible values is higher here than in any other input of the Kieffer plan. Any number of systems designs could have been used in our calculations, but because Dr. Kieffer seemed especially intrigued by a computer-managed local lesson control system, we chose to include its per course costs in our estimates. These turned out to be very high and relatively insensitive both to the number of courses converted to the use of learning equipment and to the size of Kieffer plan classes.

Next, we must determine the approximate amount of time required to staff each Kieffer plan course. Table 24 estimates time

| | 60-student classes | | |
Classes low on drill and practice	Laboratory classes	Classes high on drill and practice	Classes low on drill and practice
3	3	3	3
22	22	22	22
	60		
10	10	10	10
30	30	90	90
50	150	120	150
85	100	100	85
10	15	15	15
—	*	*	—
210	390	360	385
30	70	40	65
190	320	320	320
5	3	3	3

costs for three distinctly different kinds of courses: courses involving laboratory experiments and drill as well as learning station attendance, e.g., laboratory science courses; courses requiring little or no laboratory work but which still involve considerable practice and drill, e.g., mathematics, most languages, most social sciences, and some non-lab science courses; and courses without labs which depend less on practice and drill and more on extensive

TABLE 25
Estimated costs per class, Kieffer plan, 20- and 60-student classes

	20-student classes	
	Laboratory classes	*Classes high on drill and practice*
Staff:		
Instructors*	$ 3,710	$2,986
Assistants	217	120
Secretary	161	129
Technicians	400	
Facilities:		
Instructor's office	372	105
Assistant's office	22	12
Secretary's office	19	15
Classroom	40	30
Laboratory	350	
Other	40	
Equipment:		
Instructor's office	100	
Learning center†	3,200	3,200
Supplies and materials:		
Supplies	300	40
Software‡	700	700
Library:		
Basic share	630	630
Adjustments	(200)	(200)
Computer	1,654	330
TOTAL COSTS PER COURSE	$11,715	$8,097
TOTAL COSTS PER STUDENT	$ 586	$ 405

*Estimates include allowances for original course preparation and updating by instructor.

† Estimates include equipment rental, maintenance costs, space rental, and technical supervision.

‡ Estimates include technician salaries, space rental, secretarial support, and purchased or produced materials.

reading, e.g., philosophy, literature, history, and some fine arts appreciation courses. We have arranged the curriculum in these ways rather than in the disciplinary grouping used in previous tables in order to establish more clearly the faculty teaching loads most appropriate to this particular mode of instruction. The bottom line of the table tells the results.

With this information in hand, we have been able in Table 25

	60-student classes		
Classes low on drill and practice	*Laboratory classes*	*Classes high on drill and practice*	*Classes low on drill and practice*
$2,986	$ 4,947	$ 4,947	$4,947
120	290	160	260
129	214	214	214
	1,200		
105	469	175	175
12	29	16	16
15	25	25	25
30	100	80	80
	700		
	120		
	133		
800	3,525	3,525	1,000
40	900	120	120
450	700	700	450
630	1,890	1,890	1,890
222	(600)	(600)	666
24	4,962	990	76
$5,563	$19,604	$12,242	$9,919
$ 278	$ 327	$ 204	$ 165

to estimate the costs per class and per student enrollment of these three different kinds of courses. The first two class types, we assume, would make relatively heavy use of remote controlled learning equipment, while the last type—classes with little drill or practice—would place much heavier emphasis on the library as learning station. The results, for two different sizes of classes, reveal levels of cost implied by introduction of the Kieffer plan that are strikingly different from those to which by now we have become accustomed. Table 26 makes the comparison with other plans for classes of 20 students each.

It seems reasonable to suppose that most Kieffer plan classes would be introduced in the larger (60-student) size to permit the capture of the savings summarized in the right-hand columns of Table 25. If, then, our college were to convert approximately one-half of its normally scheduled lecture-discussion classes in the humanities and social sciences into large-sized Kieffer plan classes, and were to leave unchanged all other classes—including those in the sciences and fine arts—its annual class schedule would resemble that assumed for the programmed independent study plan. Thus, about one-third of all student enrollments would be in 54 large Kieffer plan classes concentrated in the humanities and social sciences, while the other two-thirds would be distributed widely among 162 conventional classes in all fields.

This set of assumptions yields the important conclusion that the Kieffer plan would be no more costly than the conventional plan as long as Kieffer plan classes were kept quite large. Indeed, our calculations indicate that the cost per student enrollment associated with this mixture of classes would be $227, as compared with $240 for our moderately proliferated conventional model without larger classes. The comparable figure for programmed independent study (see p. 61) would be $207. Small Kieffer plan classes would

	Laboratory science class	Social science class	Humanities class
Conventional plan	$442	$216	$201
Programmed independent study	n.a.*	173	158
Bakan plan	n.a.	247	232
Kieffer plan	586	405	278

TABLE 26 *Comparison of estimated costs per student, selected modes of instruction, 20-student class*

*n.a. = not available.

be much more expensive, however. Suppose, for example, that the same number of student registrations in the social sciences and humanities were enrolled in Kieffer plan classes averaging 20 rather than 60 students each. Then the average cost per student enrollment for *all* classes would be $277—a full 15 percent higher than a purely conventional offering. A programmed independent study plan of the same class mixture would cost only $225 (see p. 61).

The reader may wish to try his hand at calculating the costs of the Kieffer plan under alternative assumptions about class size and the spread of Kieffer plan classes through the curriculum. In general, he will find that the "break-even" class size of the Kieffer plan—that is, the size that Kieffer plan classes must be *on the average* in order to cost no more per student enrollment than normally sized conventional classes—would be in the neighborhood of 50 students. Below this figure, the Kieffer plan would be unambiguously more costly than the conventional plan. Above it, the Kieffer plan might be more efficient, depending upon the degree to which Kieffer plan classes would have replaced conventional ones and upon the sophistication of related software and hardware packages.

The Kieffer plan, we conclude, is an open option for small liberal arts colleges despite its high preparatory and facility costs. Until now, most "learning station" plans have been dismissed as far too costly for schools with limited enrollments. Our conclusions cast doubt on this viewpoint and suggest that institutions which are willing to make the necessary adjustments—especially in size of classes and number of course offerings—might find the Kieffer plan entirely feasible within reasonable budget ranges.

5. An Eclectic Plan

We have considered the costs associated with various methods of instruction. Only incidentally have we considered the cost of various combinations of these methods. Yet, in our judgment, good education calls for a mixture of various methods so that students can have varied experiences as they pursue their college careers and so that professors can teach in the manner that suits their talents and taste.

Our analysis has shown that independent study in various forms as well as tutorials are economically feasible, and it has shown that substantial savings might be achieved through Ruml plan lectures. We have also shown that great savings are possible through simplifying the curriculum and thus reducing the number of small classes. These findings lead us to the conclusion that liberal arts colleges might cut costs and at the same time improve instruction by simplifying their curricula and adopting a judicious mixture of educational methods which we call an *eclectic plan*. Such a plan would include: (1) a few large lecture courses common to all or most students; (2) courses calling for programmed independent study either with or without learning stations and mechanical systems as in the Kieffer plan; (3) courses with emphasis on tutorials; and (4) conventional classes.

The possible combinations of these various plans are almost infinite; moreover, different methods could be used in various phases of any single course. However, to test the feasibility of the eclectic plan, we have chosen a model based on certain arbitrary assumptions as follows: 35 percent of the class enrollments would be in conventional courses; 25 percent in large lecture courses; 15 percent in programmed independent study without mechanical aids; 10 percent in programmed independent study involving mechanical aids as in the Kieffer plan;[1] and 15 percent in courses involving substantial tutorial instruction as in the Bakan plan. Though we have selected arbitrary percentages, we assume that the actual distribution would be determined by the free choices of professors perhaps working under encouragement or inducements offered by the college.

We believe such a mixture of instructional modes would give a college ample opportunity for experimentation, would give students a healthy variety of educational experiences, and would give faculty members a chance to try out promising ways of teaching adjusted to their individual styles and to the needs of their subjects. In what follows, we present a cost analysis of this eclectic plan with assumed variations in curricular proliferation.

THE CURRICULUM Our survey of sample colleges permitted us in Table 14 to estimate the typical distribution of student enrollments for small independent liberal arts colleges. This information, in turn, made possible the construction of Table 27. For a college of 1,200 students and

TABLE 27 *Distribution of student enrollments by mode of instruction, eclectic plan (number of enrollments per year)*

	Modes of instruction					
Type of class	*Conventional*	*Ruml*	*Programmed independent study*	*Bakan*	*Kieffer*	*Total*
Large lecture — science		600				600
Large lecture — other		1,800				1,800
Laboratory science	480			80	80	640
Other science	200		40	40	60	340
Studio fine arts	150			30	80	260
Other fine arts	150		40	30	120	340
Languages	700					700
Social science	580		400	400	200	1,580
Humanities	1,120		960	860	400	3,340
Total student enrollments	3,380	2,400	1,440	1,440	940	9,600
Percent distribution of total	35	25	15	15	10	100

[1] The relatively small allocation to the Kieffer plan is because considerable time and experience, and possibly some technological breakthroughs, will be needed before many courses can be converted to this system.

eight-course student loads per year, it summarizes one possible arrangement of student enrollments under the eclectic plan. This is not the only arrangement possible, of course, but on the basis of testimony by our consultants as well as our own perceptions of alternative modes of instruction, we regard it as the likeliest arrangement. Note especially that the distribution of enrollments within particular modes differs one from another, reflecting our judgment that some types of classes would be more easily taught by one mode than another.

Like the conventional plan, the eclectic plan could accommodate varied degrees of course and class proliferation. Schools with diverse faculty interests and generous endowments could offer a set of course options similar to the high-proliferation model outlined in Chapter 3, keeping individual classes (except for a few large lecture courses) quite small; meagerly endowed colleges, on the other hand, might prudently choose a course list patterned after the low-proliferation model calling for substantially fewer and larger classes. A variety of other curricular options, including one we previously designated as the moderate-proliferation model, stretch out in a continuum in between. Each option, but especially those in the moderate and high range, moreover, could be modified by changing assumptions about the sectioning of large courses into smaller classes. Clearly, the options are numerous.

We have tried in Table 28 to narrow down the number of models. Thus, the table lists three distinct profiles of eclectic plan classes, similar to the low-, moderate-, and high-proliferation models of Chapter 3. Each eclectic plan model includes fewer classes than its counterpart in the pure conventional plan, of course, because of the presence in each model of several large lecture courses. In the low-proliferation model of the eclectic plan (see the upper one-third of Table 28), for example, the number of 30-student classes has been reduced from 320 to 240—a net reduction of 80 to accommodate 2,400 large lecture class registrations. Similarly, the number of 20-student classes included in the moderate-proliferation model of the eclectic plan has been reduced by 120 for the same reason. Except for these differences, the effects of constricting the curriculum of both the conventional and the eclectic plans would be the same for schools now operating in the high-proliferation range: a narrowing of choice for students and the raising of class sizes.

The number of classes offered in each proliferation model

TABLE 28 *Distribution of classes by mode of instruction, eclectic plan (number of classes per year)*

Type of class	Conven-tional	Ruml	Programmed independent study	Bakan	Kieffer	Total
A: Low-Proliferation Model						
Laboratory science	16			4	3	23
Other science	7	2	2	2	2	15
Studio fine arts	7			2	4	13
Other fine arts	8		2	1	5	16
Languages	20					20
Social science	17	2	13	12	7	51
Other humanities	36	4	31	27	12	110
Number classes	110	8	48	48	33	248
Average class size	30	300	30	30	30	39
B: Moderate-Proliferation Model						
Laboratory science	24			4	4	32
Other science	10	2	2	2	3	19
Studio fine arts	11			2	4	17
Other fine arts	12		2	2	6	22
Languages	28					28
Social science	25	2	19	18	10	74
Other humanities	57	4	48	43	20	172
Number classes	167	8	71	71	47	364
Average class size	20	300	20	20	20	26
C: High-Proliferation Model						
Laboratory science	28			5	5	38
Other science	12	2	3	3	4	24
Studio fine arts	14			3	5	22
Other fine arts	15		3	3	7	28
Languages	34					34
Social science	30	2	22	21	12	87
Other humanities	68	4	57	50	25	204
Number classes	201	8	85	85	58	437
Average class size	17	300	17	17	17	22

depends heavily upon the assumptions made about the sectioning of large courses. Table 28 was constructed on the assumption that large courses would be sectioned at 40 in the low-proliferation model, at 30 in the moderate-proliferation model, and at 25 in the high-proliferation model. These stipulations were held constant for all modes of instruction except the Ruml plan. They need not have been. Had we chosen to relax these assumptions, the eclectic plan profiles of Table 28 could have included considerably fewer classes. One possible set of alternative assumptions would section large courses of the programmed independent study and Kieffer plan modes—where latent economies of larger classes seemed highest according to Chapter 4—at twice the original number, viz., at 60 and 50, respectively, for the moderate- and high-proliferation models.[2] In that case, the totals in the lower two-thirds of Table 28 would read as follows:

	Modes of instruction					
	Conven-tional	*Ruml*	*Programmed independent study*	*Bakan*	*Kieffer*	*Total*
B: Moderate-Proliferation Model						
Number classes	167	8	56	71	35	337
Average class size	20	300	26	20	27	29
C: High-Proliferation Model						
Number classes	201	8	75	85	48	417
Average class size	17	300	19	17	20	23

COSTS OF INSTRUCTION Table 29 summarizes our estimates of the cost of implementing the eclectic plan. It was constructed in the following way: First, each type of class offered in the low-, moderate-, and high-proliferation models of Table 28 was costed-out by mode of instruction, using the techniques of cost estimation developed in Chapters 3 and 4. Next, these cost estimates were multiplied by the specified number of classes in each category and summed to produce the estimates of total instructional cost contained in column 1 of Table 29. Finally, average costs per class and per student enrollment were calculated (columns 2 and 4), based on the relative

[2] No such adjustment is proposed for the low-proliferation model because of the relatively high average class size already programmed for it in Table 28.

importance of class types within each teaching method of the eclectic plan.

The results are striking. Note, in particular, that the eclectic plan, if adopted, would cost considerably less than the conventional plan at any given level of course and class proliferation. The cost of $212 per student enrollment of its moderate-proliferation model, for example, would average 12 percent less than the $240 of a pure conventional plan curriculum with the identical degree of course proliferation (see Chapter 4). Even its costs per student enrollment at high-proliferation levels would be little more than those associated with a moderately proliferated conventional curriculum.[3]

Note, too, the dramatically different costs per student enrollment of various teaching methods used within each proliferation model. The moderate-proliferation model provides a neat illustration of these differences: Programmed independent study classes would be 65 percent more costly per student than large lecture courses, conventional and Bakan plan classes more than 150 percent more costly, and Kieffer plan classes in excess of 250 percent more expensive. These differences probably represent a truer measure of the relative costliness of various modes of instruction than the ones developed in Chapter 4, since all our earlier estimates of cost were made on the assumption that conventional plan classes would continue to dominate the college curriculum, albeit with some dilution by one or another alternative mode in instruction. These rather large differences indicate that altering our eclectic plan assumptions about the mix of instructional modes toward less costly methods of teaching like the Ruml and pro-

---

[3] Neither Chapter 4 or 5 has taken account of the costs of individualized (non-programmed) independent study, yet this mode of instruction probably is gaining ground more rapidly than any other in liberal arts colleges. We excluded it because it seemed inordinately expensive compared to other modes. To illustrate, suppose that one-third of the Bakan plan enrollments of Table 27 were taught individually rather than as part of a "class," and that five such enrollments with a single instructor made him eligible for release from one regularly sized class. For a moderately proliferated curriculum, this modest shift in the mix of instructional modes would raise total instructional costs per year by approximately $130,000 in Table 29 and it would boost overall costs per student enrollment from $212 to $226. These figures assume, of course, that the introduction of individualized reading and research courses actually would lead to teaching load relief for faculty members; traditionally, faculty members seem to have taken on such enrollments as overloads without adjustment in loads.

grammed independent study plans would produce significant reductions in total instructional costs.

An even more important source of savings for many colleges would be a reduction in the number of courses offered each year. The effects on costs of constricting the curriculum also can be seen in Table 29. Movement from a curriculum patterned after the high-proliferation model to one of moderate-proliferation would save a college $325,000 of instructional outlays annually, and a further movement to one of low-proliferation would produce $450,000 of added savings annually. Thus, even within the relatively low-cost collection of instructional modes called the eclectic

TABLE 29   *Estimated annual costs of eclectic plan by mode of instruction*

Mode of instruction	Total cost	Average cost per class	Average class size	Average cost per student enrollment
A: Low-Proliferation Model				
Ruml plan lectures	$ 239,748	$29,960	300	$100
Conventional classes	609,907	5,545	30	185
Programmed independent study classes	166,666	3,472	30	116
Bakan (tutorial) classes	315,658	6,576	30	219
Kieffer classes	244,332	7,404	30	260
Total or weighted average	$1,576,311	$ 6,345	39	$164
B: Moderate-Proliferation Model				
Ruml plan lectures	$ 239,748	$29,960	300	$100
Conventional classes	856,381	5,128	20	256
Programmed independent study classes	234,598	3,304	20	165
Bakan (tutorial) classes	373,720	5,263	20	263
Kieffer classes	331,590	7,055	20	353
Total or weighted average	$2,036,037	$ 5,593	26	$212
C: High-Proliferation Model				
Ruml plan lectures	$ 239,748	$29,960	300	$100
Conventional classes	1,008,231	5,016	17	295
Programmed independent study classes	273,945	3,222	17	190
Bakan (tutorial) classes	434,490	5,111	17	301
Kieffer classes	404,225	6,969	17	410
Total or weighted average	$2,360,639	$ 5,401	22	$246

plan, major economies would result from judicious pruning of the annual list of classes offered.

Changes in our assumptions about the sectioning of large classes, as proposed in the preceding section, would further reduce costs. The totals listed in Table 29, then, would be changed in the following ways:

	Total cost	Average cost per class	Average class size	Average cost per student enrollment
B: Moderate-Proliferation Model				
Programmed independent classes	$ 199,000	$3,535	26	$138
Kieffer classes	273,400	7,811	27	291
Total or weighted average	$1,942,249	$5,763	28	$202
C: High-Proliferation Model				
Programmed independent study classes	$ 250,450	$3,339	19	$174
Kieffer classes	344,445	7,175	20	366
Total or weighted average	$2,277,364	$5,461	23	$237

The result would be the saving of approximately $100,000 annually in either model, or about $10 per student enrollment overall.

MINIMAL COSTS These adjustments in our assumptions by no means exhaust the potential for saving of the e ⸳ctic plan. Hypothetically, the instructional program of a liberal arts college could be carried out at even lower costs by careful manipulation of other instructional variables such as average teaching loads, the rank distribution of the faculty, the intensity of facilities utilization, and the like. The effects of altering several of these variables were explored in Chapter 4 in connection with the conventional plan. It would be interesting to know how much lower the costs of instruction might be pushed in the eclectic plan, before breaching the standards of instructional quality espoused by most liberal arts colleges.

A first approximation of such a minimum might be gotten by making the following assumptions: that the college would constrict its curriculum to accord with the low-proliferation model of Table 28; that it would adopt "heavy" teaching loads for faculty as defined in Table 17; that it would strive toward a rank distribution of faculty members described in Chapter 4 as "bot-

TABLE 30 *Estimated minimum* annual costs of instruction, eclectic plan*

	Total cost	Average cost per class	Average class size	Average cost per student enrollment
Ruml plan lectures	$ 204,294	$25,530	300	$ 85
Conventional classes	469,248	4,266	30	139
Programmed independent study classes	139,918	2,914	30	97
Bakan (tutorial) classes	267,658	5,576	30	186
Kieffer plan classes	206,831	6,267	30	220
Total or weighted average	$1,287,949	$ 5,214	39	$134

*Low-proliferation model, "heavy" teaching loads, "bottom-heavy" rank distribution, and intensely utilized facilities.

tom-heavy"; and that it would raise the average utilization of classroom, studio, and laboratory space from approximately 60 to 75 percent. Changes in the scale of salaries and fringe benefits have not been proposed, however, because of the high potential of such action for lowering faculty quality.

Table 30 summarizes the costs of instruction which would be incurred under these hypothetical circumstances. Without altering average class sizes of the low-proliferation model, it shows that total instructional costs might be reduced to slightly less than $1.3 million annually, and that average costs per student enrollment would approximate $134 overall. These figures are about one-half those of the high-proliferation model in Table 29, indicating the very wide range indeed over which greater efficiency in liberal education might be practiced, even within the lower-cost eclectic plan.

6. Educational Efficiency: Some Additional Considerations

We have concentrated on the question of how an independent liberal arts college might provide education of high quality with the least average expenditure by the institution per student enrolled. This is a useful approach to educational efficiency, but it leaves out some important considerations. Our conclusions are therefore subject to several qualifications.

COSTS OF GETTING STUDENTS TO COLLEGE Higher education, as we know it, is conducted by bringing students and colleges together. The costs are of two classes: (1) those needed to get the students to college and keep them there and (2) those used to operate institutions. The total cost is the sum of these two.

Table 31 presents hypothetical (but fairly realistic) data on the typical economic cost of educating one student for one year in a private liberal arts college. As shown in this table, the costs assignable to the student are of the order of $4,600 a year; and the costs assignable to the college—to instruct him and to provide an environment conducive to his education—amount to about $4,000, or somewhat less than the amount associated with the student. The sum of the two, or total cost, is $8,600. Clearly, if in the quest for efficiency only the college portion is considered, the result is certain to miss the mark.

The major part of the cost assignable to the student is forgone earnings. This cost arises from the fact that if the student were not in college, he would probably be in the labor force. College students represent the cream of the younger generation in energy, brains, personality, and all round ability. They are eminently employable. By virtue of attending college most of them give up

TABLE 31 *Annual economic cost of educating one student in a private liberal arts college*			

Costs assignable to the student:

Expenses incident to education (books, supplies, transportation, club memberships, etc.)		$ 500		
Board and room (including summer)	$1,400			
Minus cost of board and room if student were not in college	1,200	200		
Estimated earnings if not in college	$5,000			
Minus summer and part-time earnings while in college	1,100	3,900	$4,600	

Costs assignable to the college:

Costs covered by tuition and fees (paid by student)	$2,000		
Costs covered by gifts, endowment income, etc.	2,000	$4,000*	
		$8,600	

*The $4,000 figure may be understated because colleges do not usually include depreciation of capital as a cost.

SOURCE: Adapted from Bowen, 1968.

incomes averaging $3,900 a year or more.[1] In addition, incidental expenses must be paid, averaging perhaps $700, for books, supplies, transportation, club memberships, extra cost of board and room, etc. When these incidental expenses are added to forgone income, student time in college is worth about $4,600 a year and it thus becomes a major ingredient of educational cost.

Thus each hour of student time claimed by a college is worth perhaps $3.60. It is at least as incumbent on a college to economize on this cost as to economize on faculty time or building space.

One characteristic of student time is that its cost per hour cannot be changed.[2] It is fixed by the labor market. The only way a college can economize on student time is to raise the quality of instruction so that more is learned in a given time or to shorten the time needed for a given level of achievement.

That student time is one of the costs of higher education is no

[1] If the student's alternative is not gainful employment, it is likely to be some valuable (to him) use of time such as travel, serving as housewife, leisure activities, etc.

[2] The forgone income of a student body might be changed if the composition of that student body as to background were to be altered.

new discovery. Educators, in trying to achieve efficient methods, have long considered the time of students as one of higher education's inputs along with salaries, building costs, equipment, supplies, etc. Many institutional expenditures have been made for the purpose of using student time more effectively, such as providing search service in libraries and offering assistance in computer facilities.

But many contrary examples exist which suggest that the incentive to save institutional dollars has been stronger than the incentive to save student time: Some lectures and classes are poorly prepared; orientation, registration, and final examination periods often seem inordinately long; and resistance to the shortening of baccalaureate degree periods seems strong and sometimes thoughtless.

If colleges were required to pay students for their time, as employers must do, they would be forced to seek more efficient uses of their students' time than colleges have done in the past. In fact, efficiency requires precisely that they include student time at its full value as one of the variables in determining the least costly way of achieving given educational goals.

Once the value of student time is considered, two conclusions emerge: First, when both institutional and student costs of education are counted, the total outlay is so great that nothing short of superb outcomes from the educational process can be justified or tolerated. At a total cost of $8,600 per year per student, there can be no justification for casual, slipshod, dull instruction or for a slack, spiritless academic environment. The cost of a single conventional course with 20 students is no less than $20,000.[3] An investment of this magnitude in English 102 or Mathematics 315 or Physics 182 calls for careful preparation, conscientious attention to detail, and the assurance that something significant is happening. In our opinion, few instructors are aware of the size of the investment involved in their courses. As a result, some may not feel the sense of responsibility they might if they were aware

---

[3] One class represents about one-eighth of the annual load of a student. The costs assignable to him of enrolling in a course, therefore, is $575 ($4,600 ÷ 8). The cost per student enrollment assignable to the college is $240 per course (assuming a moderately proliferated conventional curriculum). Thus the directly assignable costs per course are $16,300 ($815 × 20 students per course). Add to this the overhead institutional costs, and the grand total will be no less than $20,000.

that the cost of two or three courses—which a professor may offer in a single semester—is equal, for example, to the outlay for a substantial house.

Second, the least costly method of instruction from the point of view of the college budget may not be most efficient when student time is considered. Tradeoffs between institutional costs and student time are undoubtedly possible. For example, by increasing its expenditures per student by $500 a year, a college might offer individualized instruction that would enable students to complete the standard curriculum at a given level of quality in three years rather than four. The saving of student time over a college education would be worth $4,600; the additional cost to the college $1,500.

MARGINAL PRODUCT
Colleges compete with other parts of the economy for the labor and capital they employ. Efficiency in higher education requires that the amounts expended produce returns as great as those obtained from other "industries" such as housing, health care, or food. The requirement is not only that given resources be used as efficiently as possible, but also that the amount of resources employed be adjusted so that marginal returns from education are neither more nor less than those in other industries.

An educational institution may vary intensively the amount of resources it employs by changing the quality of instruction for a given student body, or it may vary extensively the amount of resources by changing the numbers of students enrolled. In either case, efficiency from the social point of view requires that the marginal product at both the intensive and extensive margins be equal to the marginal product from similar resources in other uses.

Judgments about the value of the marginal return from educational expenditures are difficult to make and inevitably are partially subjective. No one knows for sure the effect of the last $1,000 spent to raise quality of education for a given student body or of the last $1,000 spent to increase the number of students served. Evidence on the rates of return to investments in higher education indicate that nationally the saturation point in quality (the intensive margin) and enrollment (the extensive margin) have not yet been reached. Careful studies indicate that investments in higher education are producing a return in enhanced lifetime income of students of nearly 15 percent annually.[4] This rate of return appears to be substantially higher than that from investments in ordinary capital. If this is so, efficiency calls nationally for still greater investments in educational quality and in expanded enrollments.

It follows that one dimension of educational efficiency is to adjust expenditures in any institution so that the marginal products of the resources employed are commensurate with the marginal products of similar resources in other uses. One suspects that institutions vary in their ability to achieve satisfactory marginal returns, and that certain individual institutions may have pushed expenditures too far, into a range of returns which fall below the standard in the economy generally. Even so, the national estimates of high overall returns to educational investments suggest that most colleges are not able to attract enough resources to push the margins out to the point of social efficiency. This is a roundabout way of saying that most colleges should have more money.

STUDENT ABILITY In this study, we have assumed that the institutions under consideration are independent liberal arts colleges of better-than-average quality. This assumption implies that the students are a select group in terms of academic ability and for this reason that there is considerable latitude for experimentation with various modes of instruction involving student independence and initiative. These conditions do not exist in all institutions, and hence the results of the study may not be applicable among all liberal arts colleges — to say nothing of other branches of higher education.

It is likely that the conventional American system of higher education, with its didactic approach and its close supervision of students, evolved because educational opportunities have been extended to large numbers of students of widely varying backgrounds and social classes. Many of the students have not been academically well-prepared and many have lacked a family tradition of higher learning. As a result, instructional methods have included frequent class meetings, reliance on textbooks, use of frequent tests, mechanical counting of achievement by credits and grades, etc. European higher education, in contrast, has tended to be selective and elitist, and the instructional methods

---

[4] See for example Becker, 1964, p. 128.

have been less structured and have allowed more initiative and responsibility on the part of students.

Since World War II, for the first time in America, a few hundred institutions have become selective; that is, they have acquired student bodies with a vastly higher order of preparation and ability than ever before. Consequently, these institutions have been able to develop freer methods of instruction involving wide reading, research and other creative activity, fewer class meetings and tests, independent study, and the like. Faculty acceptance of these freer modes of instruction has grown dramatically based on the experience of working with selective student bodies.

But with the active recruitment of large numbers of minority students and with increasing efforts to widen the social classes and backgrounds represented in student bodies, instructional methods may have to revert—in part at least—to former styles. Methods depending on independent study, creative work, and student initiative may become less viable.

European experience suggests that this is so. As the diversity of student bodies in European universities has broadened, these institutions have tended to modify their instructional methods in the direction of the conventional American style.

Our conclusion is not that improvement in efficiency is impossible, but rather that claims about such improvement through student independence and initiative should be tempered by recognition that the mix of student abilities and backgrounds may be changing.

SIZE OF INSTITUTION An important factor in educational efficiency is the size or scale of the institution. For most small colleges there are potential economies to be achieved through growth in size.

As the total enrollment of a college grows, the average enrollment of classes can become larger. Even if larger courses are sectioned and some limit is placed on the size of sections, growth of enrollment can increase average size of classes by raising numbers in the less populated courses. This conclusion follows, however, only if the growth of the institution is not accompanied by proliferation of curriculum.

The effect of enrollment growth on average size of classes (and therefore on cost of instruction) may be illustrated by comparing two hypothetical colleges having identical curricula, one with 1,200 and the other with 2,400 students. The distribution of courses (not classes) by enrollment in the two institutions is assumed to be as follows:

College with 1,200 students			College with 2,400 students		
Size of course (enrollment)	*Assumed number of courses per annum*	*Number of student regis-trations*	*Size of course (enrollment)*	*Assumed number of courses per annum*	*Number of student regis-trations*
5	35	175	10	35	350
10	50	500	20	50	1,000
15	57	855	30	57	1,710
20	65	1,300	40	65	2,600
25	50	1,250	50	50	2,500
30	30	900	60	30	1,800
35	20	700	70	20	1,400
40	18	720	80	18	1,440
50	15	750	100	15	1,500
75	10	750	150	10	1,500
100	6	600	200	6	1,200
200	4	800	400	4	1,600
300	1	300	600	1	600
TOTAL	361	9,600		361	19,200
Average registration per course		26.6			53.2

Assume also that all courses are sectioned when the registration reaches 40 and that the average enrollment of such sections is 33. With these assumptions, the number of *classes* offered in the two institutions may be calculated as in the table on page 90.

If the average faculty teaching load is assumed to be five courses per annum, then 85 faculty members (or a faculty-student ratio of 1 to 14.1) would be needed in the smaller college, and 126 faculty members (or a ratio of 1 to 19) would be needed in the larger one. These results would of course be modified with variations in the assumptions. However, it is clear that growth in total enrollment would tend to reduce cost through its effect on filling small classes, *provided* the curriculum were not expanded.

In practice, the potential economy of growth is seldom realized. With growth, the curriculum tends to expand and average size of classes does not increase. (The thickness of a college catalog

Size of class	*Number of classes*	*Number of regis- trations*
College with 1,200 students		
5	35	175
10	50	500
15	57	855
20	65	1,300
25	50	1,250
30	30	900
35	20	700
Sections averaging 33	119	3,920
TOTAL	426	9,600
Average registration per class		22.5

is a good indicator of its enrollment.) Our conclusion is nevertheless valid: With curriculum given there are economies of scale, but it is equally true that with enrollment given there are economies through curricular retrenchment.

Similar analysis could be applied to other items of instructional cost, e.g., equipment such as computers, accelerators, electron microscopes, library books, pipe organs; specialized building space such as scientific laboratories, studios, swimming pools, lounges and common rooms, chapels and auditoriums; and administrative officials such as deans of students or controllers, or food directors. Many of the facilities and staff of colleges must be acquired in "lumps." Adjustments are sometimes possible, as, for example, sharing facilities with other institutions, use of part-time help, modifying educational programs to avoid big investments, buying small models of equipment, etc. But there are many instances of facilities and staff that must be acquired in chunks of irreducible size and that result in excess capacity for small colleges. In such cases growth in enrollment would entail less than proportional increases in expenditures and would result in reduced cost per student. As an institution grows from 1,200 to 2,400 enrollment, it does not necessarily need to buy a new pipe organ, or build a new stadium, or acquire another electron microscope.

In practice, however, when colleges grow, they tend to upgrade

College with 2,400 students	
Number of classes	Number of regis- trations
35	350
50	1,000
57	1,710
489	16,140
631	19,200
	30.4

their facilities and staff. They tend to harvest improved efficiency in higher quality rather than lower cost. They add to their library collections, they get bigger and better pipe organs, they upgrade their athletic facilities, they acquire bigger computers, etc., rather than spread the cost of existing facilities over more students. But there is no doubt that increasing enrollment, at least up to a point, could make possible better utilization of those facilities and staff that come in chunks of irreducible minimum size.

There are few reliable data on the relation between the size of independent liberal arts colleges and cost per student. Cost comparison for actual colleges of differing sizes do not provide much guidance on the matter because of the tendency mentioned above to upgrade facilities, increase staff, and expand the curricula as size increases. In our opinion, a useful study could be made by simulating the budgets for colleges of different sizes. In pursuing such a study one would make an inventory of the facilities, buildings, and staff needed by a college of the smallest viable size, e.g., the smallest size compatible with a faculty having "critical mass," with specialization and division of labor among administrative staff, and minimal equipment and facilities. One would then estimate the changes and additions that would be required as the hypothetical college grew in enrollment while quality of education was held constant. On the basis of such simulations one could estimate the effect on cost of changes in size and identify the optimum size from the point of view of cost per student. It is possible that at some point in growth, further increases in enrollment would be bought at the sacrifice of certain intangible qualities such as close personal relationships, attention to students, sense of community, institutional morale, etc. Many institutions might well decide in the pursuit of intangible goals to operate at an enrollment below that called for in the interests of minimum cost per student. But it would be helpful in institutional planning if reliable information were available on the relation between size and unit cost, and on the location of the minimum.

NONINSTRUC-TIONAL EX-PENDITURES OF INSTITU-TIONS

This study has been concerned primarily with efficiency in the instructional or academic portion of college budgets. In most colleges, this part of the budget is only about half the total. Therefore, efforts to improve efficiency should look to the nonacademic area as well. Indeed, if the objective is to cut costs without cutting educational quality, items in the nonacademic portions of the budget may be among the most promising candidates for reduction.

The total operating budget for a liberal arts college of the type we have used as an example in our cost calculations would look about like this:[5]

	Amount, in thousands	Percentage*
Instruction	$2,056	46%
Library	224	5
Student services	313	7
Admissions	134	3
General administration	447	10
Public relations and development	268	6
Plant operation and maintenance	536	12
Student aid	492	11
TOTAL	$4,470	100%

* These percentages are derived from several sources: a sample of 12 colleges that provided budgeting information to us; U.S. Office of Education, 1968, p. 4; 1969, pp. 12–13; Jenny & Wynn, 1971.

[5] The characteristics of such a college are set forth in Chapter 3: 1,200 students, 100 faculty members, average faculty compensation of $14,000 plus sabbaticals, teaching load of 2⅓ courses per semester, etc. It is a relatively affluent college with total operating expenditures of $3,725 per student.

Interestingly, available evidence indicates that the *percentage distribution* of expenditures among various budgetary items does not vary widely among liberal arts colleges having quite different budgets. In particular, the proportion spent on instruction (including library) seems to be near one-half for most institutions.

As shown in these illustrative figures, the noninstructional items represent about one-half the total budget. It would be short-sighted, in a drive for economy, to consider only the instructional portion. Careful studies of each noninstructional item should be made, and opportunities for saving would doubtless be discovered.

THE RICH VERSUS THE POOR One of the paradoxes of making liberal arts colleges more efficient is that rich institutions with large total budgets can afford the luxury of cost-cutting. They have built-in extravagances which can be removed without serious jeopardy to their basic programs. Poor institutions, on the other hand, have no such discretionary marginal resources. Even though they need desperately to cut cost, they cannot do so without jeopardizing their quality, their accreditation, or even their existence. Indeed, when good quality institutions do not have enough money to operate effectively, economy — from the social point of view — is not achieved by cutting total cost. It is achieved by adding to income and increasing expenditures.

Those in low-budget institutions may justly criticize this study as being unrelated to their problems. We would argue, nevertheless, that it behooves even the poorest institutions to hunt for economies. But such economies should be harvested as improvements in quality rather than as reductions in expenditure. There are few institutions that could not improve by modification of program and rearrangement of resource allocations. As we have suggested, it may in some instances be possible to improve quality while achieving economy. Indeed, we believe strongly that the rigidly structured character of most higher education and the overdependence it fosters among its students are associated with excessive expenditures and that lower cost might actually be a condition of achieving the freedom and self-reliance that are features of good education.

There is more to educational efficiency than minimizing institutional cost per student for a given quality of education and a given number of students. The time and expenses of students, the marginal product of educational expenditures, the caliber of the student body, the size of the institution, noninstructional expenditures, and the wealth of the institution must all be considered. These factors, however, in no way detract from the importance of trying to find less costly ways to operate colleges. They simply point out that many variables are involved in educational efficiency.

7. Summary and Conclusions

How might instruction be organized in a liberal arts college to reduce cost while maintaining or even improving quality? In trying to answer this question, we created a hypothetical liberal arts college with certain assumed characteristics and computed the costs of instruction with teaching conducted in a conventional manner (lecture-discussion, lecture-laboratory, and lecture-studio classes). Using these calculated costs as standards for comparison, we then modified various assumptions relating to faculty teaching loads, curricular proliferation, plant utilization, total enrollment, etc., and computed the effects on costs of these changes. Finally, we assumed various changes in the mode or system of instruction and computed their effects on costs.

The instructional systems considered (in addition to the conventional plan) were modification of the conventional plan by introducing a few lecture courses of large enrollment (a variant of the Ruml plan), programmed independent study of a type that would require minimal time of the instructor and minimal specialized equipment other than library books, tutorial instruction (the Bakan plan), programmed independent study using mechanical aids (the Kieffer plan), and a plan of our own (the eclectic plan) combining these several methods. These plans represent the principal alternatives to conventional instruction, and all are in use, at least experimentally, in many colleges.

We did not consider two modes of instruction that are gaining ground today. One of these is individualized (nonprogrammed) independent study which is clearly very expensive. The other is instruction which takes the form of work-study, internships, community involvement, etc.; the latter was omitted because this form of instruction is so varied and amorphous that it would be difficult to reach generalizations about it.

The hypothetical college we used for our computations is roughly comparable in size and characteristics to Grinnell College or Pomona College, with which the authors happen to be familiar. For many of our assumptions we relied on a survey we made of 20 liberal arts colleges from all parts of the country. The hypothetical college has 1,200 students and 100 faculty members. The average faculty teaching load is 2 courses per semester for science teachers and 2½ courses for all others. Teachers devote on the average 30 hours a week during the academic year to instruction in all its aspects. Courses carry four credits, and the typical student load is four courses per semester. The average class size is 20 students. Faculty compensation averages $14,000 including fringes with an additional allowance for the cost of sabbaticals, sick leave, etc. Physical plant costs are calculated as a rental on required space with realistic assumptions about space utilization. Substantial

	Total annual instructional cost
Highly proliferated curriculum *(450 courses offered; 570 different classes; average class enrollment of 17)*	
a. *"Heavy" faculty teaching load (6 lecture-discussion classes or 5 laboratory or studio classes per year)*	$2,332,000
b. *"Moderate" faculty teaching load (5 lecture-discussion classes or 4 laboratory or studio classes per year)*	2,683,000
c. *"Light" faculty teaching load (4 lecture-discussion classes or 3 laboratory or studio classes per year)*	3,206,000
Moderately proliferated curriculum *(335 courses offered; 476 different classes; average class enrollment of 20)*	
a. *"Heavy" faculty teaching load*	1,985,000
b. *"Moderate" faculty teaching load*	2,280,000*
c. *"Light" faculty teaching load*	2,714,000
Compressed (low proliferation) curriculum *225 courses offered; 320 different classes; average class enrollment of 30)*	
a. *"Heavy" faculty teaching load*	1,430,000
b. *"Moderate" faculty teaching load*	1,628,000
c. *"Light" faculty teaching load*	1,923,000

TABLE 32 *Costs of conventional instruction with varying assumptions about curricular proliferation and faculty teaching loads*

* Standard plan used as base for comparison.

sums are allocated to the library and computer facilities. The curriculum is considerably less proliferated than that actually found in most colleges of the type we surveyed.

Our effort to determine how the direct cost of instruction in this hypothetical college would be affected by variations in the way instruction is conducted was constrained by two conditions: first, that quality of education must be maintained or improved; and, second, that faculty members not be expected to devote more than 30 hours a week during the academic year, or about 960 hours a year, to instruction, the remainder of their time being reserved for scholarly work, participation in the affairs of the college, and other professional activities.

Cost was expressed as total cost of instruction, cost per class offered, and cost per student course enrollment. The principal results of the calculations are shown in Tables 32 to 37.

Cost per class offered	Cost per student course enrollment
$4,092	$243
4,707	280
5,623	334
4,170	208
4,789*	240*
5,702	285
4,468	149
5,087	170
6,009	200

TABLE 33   *Costs of conventional instruction with varying assumptions about classroom utilization and numbers of students*

	Total annual instructional cost	Cost per class offered	Cost per student course enrollment
Classroom utilization			
(Moderately proliferated curriculum; moderate teaching load)			
a. Intense classroom utilization (37 hours per week, lecture-discussion classrooms; 27 hours per week, science and fine arts classrooms; 22 hours per week, studios and laboratories)	$2,248,000	$4,721	$236
b. Moderate classroom utilization (25, 18, and 15 hours per week, respectively)	2,280,000*	4,789*	240*
c. Low classroom utilization (18, 13, and 11 hours per week, respectively)	2,312,000	4,856	244
Numbers of students			
(Moderately proliferated curriculum; moderate teaching load)			
a. Student body of 1,200 (average class size of 20)	2,280,000*	4,789*	240*
b. Student body of 1,800 (no increase in number of courses; average class size of 30)	2,456,000	5,159	172

*Standard plan used as base for comparison.

In making all these calculations, we were mindful of the condition that educational quality must not be sacrificed—and if possible should be raised. We have no factual evidence about the effect of changes in mode of instruction upon quality or effectiveness of education. We have only our own judgments, and anyone else is entitled to make different ones.

Our opinion is that each of the variations and plans we have studied is worthy of consideration. We believe it is possible in some cases to increase the course load of faculty without exceeding the work standard we set, namely, 30 hours a week during the academic year (or 960 hours per year) devoted to instruction in all its aspects. We firmly believe that nothing but good could come from simplification of the curriculum. We believe that modest economies without harm to education might result from achieving a balanced distribution of faculty by rank, from adjusting the curriculum so that expensive subjects of low priority are weeded

TABLE 34 *Costs of conventional instruction with varying assumptions about rank distribution of faculty and course distribution by subjects*

	Total annual instructional cost	Cost per class offered	Cost per student course enrollment
Rank distribution of faculty (Moderately proliferated curriculum; moderate teaching load)			
a. Top-heavy rank distribution (64 percent associate professors and professors; average compensation $14,610	$2,338,000	$4,910	$246
b. Average rank distribution of 20-college sample (52 percent associate professors and professors; average compensation $14,000)	2,280,000*	4,789*	240*
c. Bottom-heavy rank distribution (30 percent associate professors and professors; average compensation $11,750)	2,035,000	4,275	214
Course distribution by subjects (Moderately proliferated curriculum; moderate teaching load)			
a. Average distribution of courses by subject (20-college sample)	2,280,000*	4,789*	240*
b. Ten percent reduction in number of more costly courses and correspondingly more of less expensive types	2,251,000	4,729	236

* Standard plan used as base for comparison.

out, and from improving the utilization of plant. In some cases, economies could be achieved without hurting education through expansion of total enrollment. If several or all of these things could be done at the same time, savings in instructional costs of the order of a quarter to a third should be attainable.

The Ruml plan strikes us as a highly promising innovation. It was proposed about 15 years ago and to date has made small impact. It was offered, however, at a time when colleges were not much interested in economy. Its time may now have come. We recommend it not as an institutionwide panacea but as a likely use for a portion of the teaching load, possibly one-fourth. The lecture method has some virtues when it is in the hands of competent lecturers. And there is much to be said, from the point of view of collegiality, in having large numbers of students share identical

TABLE 35 *Costs of conventional instruction under a combination of assumptions producing minimum cost including the Ruml plan*

	Total annual instructional cost	Cost per class offered	Cost per student course enrollment
Conventional plan with minimum cost			
(Compressed curriculum; heavy faculty teaching load; bottom-heavy rank distribution of faculty; intinsive classroom utilization; mix of courses weighted toward less expensive subjects)	$1,223,000	$3,821	$127
Ruml plan			
(One-fourth of all instruction concentrated in 8 large lecture classes)			
a. Moderately proliferated curriculum (remainder of curriculum, 356 classes, taught by conventional methods with average enrollment of 20; moderate teaching load)	1,940,000	n.a.*	202
b. Minimum cost curriculum (assumptions as above for conventional plan plus 8 large lecture classes)	1,126,000	n.a.	117
c. Conventional plan (for comparison)	2,280,000†	4,789†	240†

* n.a. = not available.
† Standard plan used as base for comparison.

educational experiences. But the big virtue of the plan is, as Mr. Ruml pointed out, that it enables an institution to deliver a substantial block of instruction very inexpensively and thus to husband resources for more individualized types of instruction. Seminars, independent study, new forms of mechanized instruction, and the like can be afforded if some instruction can be delivered satisfactorily at low cost.

We believe there is a bright future for independent study of a kind which increases the self-reliance of the student and requires and equips him to learn independently, with a minimum of dependence upon instructors. We have explored three types of independent study: programmed independent study without equipment except books; the Kieffer plan, which emphasizes mechanical equipment; and the Bakan plan, which uses tutorials. These three are really quite similar. We found all three to be economically feasible, though none was a big money saver. We learned that these schemes are viable, however, only if the independent study

TABLE 36 *Cost of instruction under three different plans: programmed independent study, tutorial (Bakan plan), and independent study with mechanical aids (Kieffer plan)*

	Total annual instructional cost	Cost per class offered	Cost per student course enrollment
Programmed independent study plan			
(Requires no specialized equipment except books; requires minimal time of teacher except preparation of program and general supervision; courses conducted in groups to minimize need for private interviews; "heavy" faculty teaching load)			
a. Moderately proliferated curriculum (476 classes per year, about one-third converted to programmed independent study; average class size of 20 students)	$2,138,000	$4,491	$225
b. Compressed curriculum (292 conventional classes averaging 20 students; 54 independent study classes averaging 50 students)	1,999,000	n.a.	207
c. Conventional plan (for comparison)	2,280,000*	4,789*	240*
Tutorial instruction (Bakan plan)			
(400 classes per year; languages, science, and studio courses taught conventionally; all other courses taught as tutorials; "light" faculty teaching load)	2,196,000†	5,480	261†
Independent study with learning stations and mechanical aids (Kieffer plan)			
(Requires expensive teaching-learning equipment; requires heavy preparation of program but relatively light teaching loads while course is in progress; mix of conventional and independent study courses same as above in programmed independent study)			
a. Moderately proliferated curriculum	2,636,000	5,537	277
b. Compressed curriculum	2,177,000	n.a.	277

*Standard plan used as basis of comparison.

† Total costs are lower than for the conventional plan, and cost per student course enrollment is higher because the Bakan plan requires students to enroll in fewer courses during the junior and senior years than conventionally.

is programmed for sizable groups of students, and if groups of students take the independent study courses with a common schedule. If independent study becomes completely individualized —that is, if each student's program is unique and the student consults the professor individually and is examined individually— the cost becomes exorbitant. To organize a group of students to work together on the same schedule appears to be a condition

TABLE 37 *Costs of instruction under an eclectic plan*

	Total annual instructional cost	Cost per class offered	Cost per student course enrollment
Standard eclectic plan			
(Assumes 35 percent of instruction in conventional plan classes, Ruml plan 25 percent, programmed independent study 15 percent, Kieffer plan 10 percent, and Bakan (tutorial) plan 15 percent)			
a. Highly proliferated curriculum	$2,361,000	$5,401	$246
b. Moderately proliferated curriculum	2,036,000	5,593	212
c. Compressed curriculum	1,576,000	6,345	164
Minimum cost eclectic plan			
(Compressed curriculum; heavy faculty teaching load; bottom-heavy rank distribution of faculty; intensive classroom utilization; mix of courses weighted toward less expensive subjects)	1,288,000	5,214	134
Conventional plan (for comparison)	2,280,000*	4,789*	240*

* Standard plan used as base of comparison.

of economic feasibility if live professors are to have a substantial part in the instructional process. Educationally, we should make a virtue out of this economic need for groups of students to be working on the same schedule. We should contrive to encourage them to learn independently not only as individuals but also as groups who are working together independent of the professor and learning from one another. Independent study need not be a wholly solitary endeavor.

We conclude that there is no one best way of education suitable for all institutions, all subjects, all professors, and all students. We reject any single plan in favor of an eclectic plan that draws on conventional lecture-discussions and lecture-laboratories, large lectures, independent study, tutorials, and mechanized instruction. We find that the eclectic plan is economically feasible. We believe there is ample opportunity within prevailing economic constraints for bold educational experimentation. We also believe that faculty discussions of educational policy should be more attuned to budgetary considerations than they have been traditionally. The curriculum, the mode of instruction, and the teaching load do make a difference in costs. They may not spell the difference between institutional solvency and bankruptcy, but they may differentiate between institutional progress and stagnation.

Appendix A: Toward a System of Individually Taught Courses

Jarold A. Kieffer

PURPOSE The purpose of this paper is to describe the objectives and the methodology of teaching college courses on an individual rather than a mass basis, and to suggest means for moving toward such a system.

BACKGROUND Commonly, small liberal arts colleges in their literature stress that they offer excellence of teaching, small [sic] teacher-pupil ratios, ample contact between teachers and students, curricular flexibility, and many opportunities for independent study. Unfortunately, in actual practice, a number of these educational features are not consistently realized, and in some cases they are not realized at all.

The gap between aspiration and realization is particularly wide in the area of teaching methodology. As will be seen below, the direct and indirect consequences of this gap are both substantial and serious. For one thing, many of the students who come to the small colleges become disillusioned when they realize that they are not getting the kind of educational experience they may have been led to expect, and their parents begin to have doubts as to why they should pay the much higher tuition costs than they would if their son or daughter went to a public institution.

Although class enrolments at the liberal arts colleges may vary from sparse to heavy, broad ranges of their curriculum are at present taught through a traditional mass-lecture presentation, plus some amount of question-and-answer give and take. Often the students are expected to supplement the classwork by readings. The readings are designed to provide greater depth in some of the subject matter presented or to afford the student a chance to

NOTE: The material in Appendix A is reprinted with permission from *Liberal Education,* October 1970.

become familiar with different viewpoints or other perspectives concerning it. In addition, students may do term papers on subjects related to each course. Nearly all students take a final examination, and some professors give periodic or mid-term examinations.

PROBLEM   Many of the small liberal arts institutions have experienced the pressure of larger enrolments. Also, through the constant and almost "built-in" faculty tendency to curricular proliferation, the pressure for additional staffing and higher teaching costs is never-ending. However, since budgetary and recruiting deficiencies are usually chronic in all institutions, the end result is that the teacher-pupil ratios repeatedly improve and then erode again.

Whether for reasons of increased enrolments or staff deficiencies, or for other causes, we see continued evidence over much of the college scene that the amount of interaction between teachers and classes is tending to shrink. This shrinkage then throws greater pressure on the mass lectures and outside reading as means for the students to become familiar with the content of their courses. More and more students are left to sit and listen passively in day after day of classes.

These tendencies are not only troublesome on their own, but take on an even more difficult aspect when we consider the inherent weaknesses of the mass-lecture method.

The mass-lecture method as a teaching technique obviously has some advantages, but in many respects the disadvantages are greater. For instance, the method emphasizes constant attention on the part of the student, together with a facility with the pencil. A good wrist becomes as important as a good ear.

However, learning should always emphasize thought progression or chain reactions. In other words, a student should be encouraged to reflect on the idea relationships, fundamental principles, or insights that are identified or start to be identified as a consequence of exposure to the content. These free-association processes are sharply inhibited when the student must discipline his mind and wrist in order to keep up with the lecturing professor. If his mind wanders in reflection, and he begins putting two and two together on something the professor said, or on something he is relating from another class, he does so at his own peril. He risks getting behind, feels the frustration of being paced, and loses what might be an exciting learning moment.

The mass-lecture method also is disadvantageous in that it fails to recognize that individual students come to the class with different starting points and capacities. Instead of being able to proceed through the content at their own speed, they are artificially frozen into the uniform pace that the professor must establish and which he usually does in accordance with some common denominator of class capacity.

The mass-lecture method is particularly wasteful when it is used for imparting to the students masses of data and other information that the students could be expected to master on their own. Moreover, the whole mass-lecturing approach is yet another unfortunate part of an educational system that compels the student to deal with the content of his courses on a "then and now," "take it or leave it" basis.

Instead of being able to concentrate his time and energy on the mastery of particular course contents at a given time, the student's time and attention is fragmented. He faces in rapid hourly succession, for days and weeks on end, a series of unrelated presentations by the professors of his various classes. He must capture all these bits and pieces in his notes or his memory, try to organize his experience in some continuity pattern for each subject, and be tested thereon at some future date.

Here also the system is defective. The sheer numbers of students force the professors to use either objective, multiple-choice test questions (which have real limitations as far as revealing mastery of the contents and ability to employ the knowledge and understanding effectively), or they can use a few essay or problem questions, the answers to which can only be a relatively small sample of what the student has actually learned.

Worse yet, even within these limitations, very few professors have time to check their own performance as a direct factor in student performance. When the students rise from a lecture, the professor usually has not the slightest basis for judging what each student has absorbed that day, and neither he nor the student has time to find out.

Additionally, the whole mass-lecture system reinforces the tendency of the students to cram knowledge, regurgitate it and forget it. The students who pass a course move on to other courses. They don't have the luxury of time or ready means for review or correction of weaknesses. They are locked into rigid course periods, schedules, sequences and terms or semesters that force them on to the next hurdle, ready or not. When each academic term ends, both students and professors simply get ready for the next term with scarcely a backward look.

This "up or out" people-squandering system starts in the elementary grades and proceeds throughout the entire secondary and college levels. It is a ruthless and incredibly inefficient system that permits and almost forces weaknesses to go undetected or uncorrected, that piles weakness upon weakness, that shoves students on to ever more complex educational content without real information on their mastery of prior foundation content. As an input system, it is disintegrative rather than integrative.

TOWARD AN IMPROVED SYSTEM Professors have long marked and deplored the weaknesses and gaps they find in student performance, but somehow efforts to discover the root causes or to correct the problem seem to languish. Obviously, reform of the above described system will be very difficult, time-consuming and costly. But change we must.

We are literally in a race between the tuition-paying public's growing hostility to the steady increase in educational costs, on the one hand, and the ever-increasing demand and need for more effective educational experiences on the other.

Clearly, we need to begin working toward a different educational system that emphasizes the following objectives:

1 Mastery of educational content rather than steady progress over a series of arbitrarily established time hurdles;

2 Movement of students through educational content on an individual basis at their own best pace;

3 More emphasis on integrative rather than disintegrative learning experiences and learning environments;

4 More efficient use of student and teacher time;

5 Wide options in teaching methods to accomplish specific teaching tasks;

6 Enlarged and more efficient opportunities for students to work with their professors and seek their help;

7 More efficient use of college facilities;

8 Constant validation of teaching methods and educational content as reflected in ability of each student to demonstrate mastery of desired contents.

PROPOSAL Once a student has been approved for a program of academic preparation he should be enabled to advance through the content at his own best pace. Also, he should be able to direct his efforts selectively, taking certain related courses in direct succession or simultaneously in clusters, so as to maximize interrelationships and to encourage and conserve learning momentum. Such a system of individual pacing and subject clustering would help reduce boredom, distraction or anxiety. It might liberate many hours for pursuit of the student's other academic interests. At the very least, it would give to students an alternative to the thought-disintegrating effects of the present term-long series of fifty-minute classes on unrelated subjects.

Instead of coming to a lecture hall, the student would come to a learning station. The learning station would consist of facilities for the presentation of course content by the most desirable methods for presenting that content, e.g., video tapes, films, printed material, reading texts. Some of the content might best be presented graphically through charts and diagrams in order to demonstrate the sequential impact of some phenomena or development. Films or video tapes could be used to demonstrate and explain certain kinds of actions or settings.

On entering the learning station the student would indicate to the attendant the course he proposed to pursue at that time. He would be given a "book," which in its introduction would describe the set of sequences into which the course was divided, the skills to be taught or developed, the desired understandings to be achieved in each phase of the course, and the supplemental readings and other library references considered material to the course.

Guided by instructions on how to proceed, the student would then move through the programmed sequences or phases one by one, in each case demonstrating mastery over one phase before proceeding to the next.

The student would set his own pace. He would do this by determining not only when to come to the learning station, but how long to stay there. While there, he could control the equipment in such a way that he could hold a chart in front of him indefinitely while he studied it. He could reverse the presentation in order to review something heard or seen before. He could replay material over and over again if he felt dissatisfied with his grasp of something. If he didn't happen to feel well or couldn't focus his mental faculties at any given point, he could simply return at another time. The learning stations would be open all hours of the day, into the evening, and on weekends.

When the student felt that he had a satisfactory comprehension of Phase I of a course, he, together with others who were at that same point, would meet with the instructor for formal discussions, questions and answers, and additional perspectives. These sessions would give the students a chance to react directly with their instructor as well as with their fellow students as they all moved through the content. Students could also see their instructors at other times if they were not comprehending the instructions, or the presentations, or if some more urgent line of questions needed to be pursued. The instructor could help the student to determine whether indeed he had a satisfactory comprehension of Phase I.

Each student who had completed Phase I would then take a test on its content. He would be judged on the following basis: "A," "B," "C" or "Not yet." The purpose of this test would not be to establish a recorded grade, but merely to inform him and the instructor as to whether he had a satisfactory comprehension of Phase I. If he did, he would move to Phase II. If he did not, he would be informed of the manner in which his comprehension was deficient. He would then address himself to the content once again, concentrating on developing a mastery of the areas in which he was previously deficient. Moving at his own pace, he could stay with Phase I as long as he wished or needed to.

The emphasis throughout would be on individual mastery of the content rather than on the "take it or leave it right now" situation that has evolved from our mass-lecture and fifty-minute class system.

The tests given at the end of each phase would also serve another purpose. Over time, an analysis of their results might help pinpoint for the instructor weaknesses in the presentation. In other words, if the students, as indicated by their test reactions or oral comments in the seminar sessions or otherwise, seemed unable to grasp some presentation of the content, the instructor could then investigate the reasons why. He might conclude that a particular part of the content needed a different kind of presentation. Or, he might decide that his questions on that content presentation were weak or misleading. Through this constant validation system, the educational soundness of the whole content presentation could be continually tested.

After the student had proceeded phase by phase through the content of the course, and had his seminars or other sessions with the instructor and with other students, he then would take a comprehensive examination. This would become the basis for his final grade unless special readings, reports or term papers were also involved.

Obviously, because of the random timing of these final examinations, professors would have to maintain variable question patterns to avoid the effects of prior knowledge of the test questions. Or they might devise take-home tests that put the emphasis on use and integration of the course content rather than memorization.

Before the final comprehensive examination, the student could go to the learning station at his own convenience and review all or any part of the content. He would determine when he was ready to take the final examination. Again, the grading system would be "A," "B," "C" and "Not Yet." Those in the "Net Yet" category would not have this reflected in their transcript. They could take the course again simply by re-registering. They could then be given a clear indication of where they were weak and could concentrate their further efforts on overcoming their specific deficiencies.

A METHOD OF STARTING The individually-taught learning system has several advantages over prior efforts at introducing computer-assisted or audio-visual-centered courses. Often these efforts either eliminated a flesh-and-blood professor and the students' relationship to him, or they supplanted a local professor with some off-campus "star" whose lectures were canned and imported.

Such endeavors did not get at the root problems involved in much of our current teaching methodology. Even if the student sees before him a filmed, closed-circuit TV or video-taped version of a professor rather than a live one, he is still attempting to learn in a mass-lecture context. He still faces a bewildering and often unrelated series of fifty-minute classes and moves at an arbitrarily established pace rather than his own. Moreover, the whole idea of relying on canned, closed-circuit or imported lectures adds distance between students and teachers and creates insecurities and resentments among faculties who feel that their jobs will be displaced by films and so-called "stars."

A different and necessarily slower method of proceeding will produce better long-range results consistent with the eight objectives stated earlier. It is better to enlist local faculty support through encouragement rather than through actions that could lead to alienation and insecurity.

The individually-taught learning system has the advantage that it can be started on a course-by-course basis rather than through a revolution of the entire curriculum. A start could be made by identifying several professors who, with direct financial assistance, would be willing to convert their courses to the individually-taught method. In other words, use could be made of a voluntary approach rather than a mandatory one where every professor might feel that he was being compelled to change his whole academic pattern and style.

The number of volunteer professors could be encouraged to grow each year until, eventually, broad ranges of the curriculum would have been converted to the new system. Professors preferring not to convert would simply continue to teach their courses in whatever manner they chose, consistent with the over-all needs of their departments.

Over time, and certainly in regard to elective courses, the students would be exercising their own preferences on teaching methodology, and both the administration and the faculty would naturally evaluate the whole faculty-student experience in order to shape future directions.

Meaningful progress in developing individually-taught courses will depend on the assembling of a number of resources. Each course that is to be taught in this manner will require (a) an instructor or instructors who would be in over-all charge of development; (b) the services of an educational psychologist experienced in learning behavior; and (c) an audio-visual programmer. The program development in each case will of necessity take as much as a year, assuming full-time staff participation.

Program development would be initiated by a process in which the development team would analyze the content of the course and then determine the educational objectives. In other words, the team would first determine the kinds of knowledge and understanding as well as experience it wants the students to have on completion of each phase. When these objectives were determined, the next step would be to select the best method of presentation of each part of the content in the light of the educational objectives and learning behaviors. Experiments with different methods of presentation would be necessary, and tests could be made with student volunteers to determine results.

Finally, determinations would be made as to the kind of audio-visual hardware and physical arrangements that would be most harmonious with the program objectives. These determinations would lead to both programmatic and budgetary calculations that could then be presented to the college administration for consideration.

At least a year of testing would be necessary following activation of each course.

This whole process could yield some immediate benefits even where an institution might not be able to afford the audio-visually equipped learning stations at the outset.

Once a professor had gone through the type of course analysis described above, he could probably identify significant parts of the content that could be handled by the students through private reading. After he made clear what he expected each of them to do, he then could reorganize his time and student contact periods along the more efficient seminar lines contemplated in the overall proposal noted above.

Such a limited approach would not permit as much learning method experimentation as would the more extensive audio-visual approach, but, even so, it could provide a ready way to quicken the pace of teaching-learning reform which has languished for so long. Moreover, the very process of encouraging and facilitating the efforts of professors to make a critical content-presentation and learning-behavior analysis of their courses could open up broad new perspectives for them in recasting content and experimenting with different forms of presentation.

GENERAL CAMPUS IMPLICATIONS
The adoption of individually-taught courses on an extensive basis could eventually have sweeping implications for the whole pattern of student and faculty life and campus development.

Teaching courses on an individual basis would open up a whole new method of handling enrolments. If it were applied widely on a campus, the present complicated system of deploying students to specific hourly lecture and discussion sections would be done away with.

By systematic use of learning stations, many bright students could master their courses in two or three years rather than four and so reduce the cost of their undergraduate education. Other students might take more time for a course that gives them trouble, but they might make up the time in courses that come easier. More people could be taught in less time, and they could each arrange their time more efficiently. Obviously, these advantages could have real meaning to small liberal arts colleges as they struggle with inadequate staffs and resources and face the problem of rising costs and constantly eroding teacher-pupil ratios.

A student would no longer have to worry about the wasteful problem of being too late to take the beginning course in a three-course sequence. All courses would be available at all times in the learning stations. In addition, a student who did unsatisfactory work in the first of a three-course sequence need not worry about wasting a whole year thereafter. He would be able to take the first course over at any time, concentrating only on his weak spots, and be in a position to take his qualifying exam at any time he felt he had remedied his deficiencies. Then he could go on to the second course of the sequence at any time. Also, he need not by stymied by being unable to get into a prerequisite course before taking a follow-up sequence. The prerequisite course always would be available.

Professors also would be benefited by the individually-taught system. Rather than giving as much time as they do now to mass lectures they and their students would spend their time more effectively in small informal sessions, raising questions with each other and probing for understanding. Student advising would occur more gradually through the year rather than in an enormous crush a few times a year.

Ultimately, the term or semester system could be eliminated for much of the student body and faculty, and the peaks and valleys of course preparation and term-paper and examination reading could be evened out.

New kinds of testing systems, employing teaching machines, already exist. These might be employed to help reduce the testing burden on professors.

Summer terms could become a regular part of the academic year, and professors could be given several months each year to rework, update and correct their teaching materials in the learning stations. A teaching year might include nine months of seminar classes, two months of "retooling" relatively minor changes in course presentation, and one month's vacation. Necessarily, sabbaticals would have to occur more frequently than once every seven years, and they would become a regular institutionally-financed part of staff development. For instance, once each three or four years, professors would be helped to undertake more substantial changes in their presentation, as necessary. They could also seek broadening experiences, publish books or reports, do research work, or carry on other activities that would enhance their value as teachers.

Capital construction on the campuses would also be affected substantially by the individually-taught system. Classrooms that are empty much of the time could be converted to learning stations and seminar-type rooms. Much higher utilization ratios could be achieved, and space could be used more efficiently. Learning stations could be located conveniently near to dormitories and other living accommodations so as to encourage usage broadly spread throughout the day, evenings and weekends.

CONCLUSIONS   The potentialities of an individually-taught course system are extensive. Obviously, such innovations would require careful experimentation and testing over time. But the alternative of simply proceeding as we are now is neither desirable nor really possible.

Without drastic changes in the way we deal with the students' demands for better educational experiences or with deteriorating teacher-pupil ratios, and considering the chronic inadequacy of funds, many of our institutions face a drop in quality to unacceptable levels, a growing frustration of faculty and staff, and an explosive student morale problem. The steadily rising costs of a good college education can only exasperate the tuition-paying public and complicate the efforts of college trustees and administrators to secure essential philanthropic support.

We have no time to lose in stating the urgent case for change and for securing the kind of seed money that will be required to commence the kinds of new teaching arrangements outlined above.

Appendix B: Individual Learning Systems

Jarold A. Kieffer

The purpose of this memorandum is to outline my conceptions of a typical learning center for courses in various fields.

I suppose the first thing to say is that I have not conceived of the learning centers as doing all things alike for all courses. This would be manifestly unwise, as well as infeasible.

Basically, my concept of individual learning rests on the fact that a substantial portion of any course is essentially informational or data processing intake, and it is very inefficient and educationally destructive for the professor to handle that portion of the content by lecture methods. I am suggesting that we urge the professors to distinguish the basic informational or data processing components of their content and arrange for the student to input these components on his own time and at his own pace.

The professor would then use his time with individual students or groups of students as they go through each of the informational phases. In these group or individual sessions, the professor and students would discuss the content examined thus far; deal with the more subjective aspects of the content, such as value judgments; raise additional questions; and probe for understanding. Obviously, the phasing is somewhat arbitrary and would vary according to the nature of the course. Likewise, the character of the informational input would vary as between courses.

For instance, in a chemistry course the student might be asked to do anything from trying to understand densities to working out a laboratory experiment that demonstrates the effects of chemical interaction. Necessarily, that would be quite different from what the student would be asked to do in a course on poetry. There, for instance, the professor might program into the learning station a variety of writing styles to show comparative structural schemes. Or he might wish to have the student examine how different poets use symbolism. Listening equipment could be used to demonstrate the relative impact of the written versus the spoken word. Or it might be used to demonstrate how different speaking styles affect meaning.

In all the areas listed, an incredible number of professors today are still trying to handle these phases by lectures or by assigning required reading or by combinations of both.

By way of an example of a social science course handled through individual learning centers, I might, for instance, describe how one of my public administration classes—the one on the Presidency— might be handled.

As the instructor, I would program into the learning center some reading and diagramming concerning the nature of the chief executive position under discussion by the Founding Fathers in the Constitutional Convention of 1787. Specifically, what were the different views as expressed in the convention on the alternative roles contemplated for the proposed chief executive? Remember, in the then existing government under the Articles of Confederation, there was no chief executive. The students would be shown how things were conducted without a chief executive, and what the apparent consequences were that led to demands among many of the members of the convention that there be a chief executive.

Next, the students, by appropriate descriptions and diagrams, would be exposed to the various alternative chief executive concepts then existing in the world. They would be asked to consider what we know about the answers to the perennial questions: Why a chief executive? How do various societies choose their leadership? How do they handle the question of leadership succession? The students would be shown the alternatives debated by the convention.

Next, the students would be asked to study in detail Article II of the Constitution in order to see what the Founding Fathers finally agreed upon by way of a chief executive and his powers. Through the use of films and diagrams, each of the powers of the presidency as then envisioned in the United States of 1787 would be brought to life, and the then intended meaning of each power discussed.

Next, the content would deal with what George Washington and his successors did to give flesh-and-blood reality to Article II of the Constitution. The students would be asked to examine the administrative development of the executive against a backdrop of leadership and internal-external events. The dramatically contrasting styles and concepts of the Presidency as between a Washington and a Jefferson would be revealed and examined. The student would be given examples of how political mobilization became a handmaiden for the exercise of executive leadership.

Next, the student would examine the growing institutionalization of the role of the President against a backdrop of causes. This process would be brought up to date, and an analysis would be made of the impact of the Budget and Accounting Act of 1921 in terms of the potential it created for presidential leadership. Comparably, the Depression would be examined in terms of its implications for the enormous expansion of the role of the federal government, and the built-in consequences that had for the role of the chief executive of that vastly expanded layer of government.

Next, the content would help the student understand the setting of the Presidency today, and a delineation would be made of the chief and continuing roles of the President, whether he does them well or poorly.

A student would have a chance to examine the evolution of the Presidential staff arms in terms of the attempts of various Presidents to carry out their assorted roles. Leadership styles would be contrasted against a backdrop of evolving national moods and problems, and the student would have a chance to examine the ways in which each President attempted to react to his leadership and administrative problems. In this connection, the student would be shown quotes from the Presidents about their reactions, as well as their proposals for change in the presidential system.

Finally, the student would examine the strengths and deficiencies in the present system as it has evolved, and he would be given a chance to try to estimate the probable future direction of the Presidency as a consequence of the nature of the problems yet to be dealt with, the complexities of administration, the changing political complexion of the country, and the growing incapacity of the federal government to achieve meaningful results in the matter of dealing with urban crises.

I envision a whole range of audio-visual techniques for revealing or demonstrating in a realistic way the How and Why of many of the above contents. Film clips, chartings that demonstrate evolution of organizational patterns, video tapes that contrast leadership styles—all these and other audio-visual demonstrations could be vastly effective in helping students comprehend more than they are able to by simply listening to a professor talk or reading a book. Clearly, we need a combination of all these methods, each used to best advantage for particular parts of the content.

Throughout the course, students would move at their own pace through the informational components, and those who have completed designated phases would meet for phase-end seminars with the professor. Here, they would ask questions that they felt were either not dealt with in the presentation or developed in relation to it, or because of it. Also, these group sessions would give the students a chance to argue out value problems with each other and gain insight into how others reacted to the content of the course thus far experienced on an individual basis.

The professor would have a chance to probe to see if the students really comprehended the intended content. Obviously he would also check to see if the learning station materials were useful to the students and achieved their intended learning outcomes.

Appendix C: Obstacles to Curricular and Teaching-Learning Innovation in Higher Education

Jarold A. Kieffer

One cannot examine the national experience with curricular and teaching-learning reform and innovation in higher education without coming to the conclusion that the successes seem to be incredibly few, or at least still inconclusive, while the failures are many. When one questions and probes the reasons for this outcome, he is struck by the similarity of the factors that seem to determine why failure occurs.

From these discussions and observations, I have set down the apparent obstacles to curricular and teaching-learning innovation in higher education. (These are not listed in any special order of priority.)

1. LACK OF FACULTY INCENTIVE The faculty promotion and tenure reward system simply does not provide "points" for efforts spent in creative activity in teaching or in the matter of curricular reform. Faculty members, especially the younger ones, certainly up to recently, have felt that the essential ingredients of academic success related more to national professional recognition than to local campus performance and service. Moreover, by and large, they concluded that such national recognition was earned largely through the route of disciplinary research and scholarly activity evidenced by publication in national professional journals. For prestige reasons, most departments, schools, and colleges and universities accepted this conclusion; and their written or de facto promotion and tenure systems still are substantially oriented toward evidence of national professional recognition.

Closely linked to this reward system is the fact that young professors are especially interested in their potential standing in the national hiring market, and this hiring market also relates itself primarily to evidences of recognition by the national profession.

Few of the national professions have tended to emphasize or reward creative activity in teaching or curriculum development.

Hence, faculty members, when considering investing time in either pedagogical or curriculum reform measures or innovations, tend to conclude that they had better invest their time in research and publication of national professional interest.

Despite many current protestations that the above-described value system does not apply on this or that campus, it is simply a fact of life and operates in the minds of the young faculty members as a fact of life, whether or not the university and college administrations and departmental leaderships think or say otherwise.

2. POOR FACULTY MORALE The present higher education scene can almost be summarized in the word "challenge"—not challenge in the opportunity sense, but challenge in the authority sense. The whole posture and function of the faculty is under challenge. The time-honored tribal customs of the faculty are no longer honored. The students are challenging the faculty. The outer public, including trustees, legislators, and public executives, also have found the faculty to be a happy target for criticism and abuse.

Now too, higher education administrators are coming to feel that faculty habits and faculty opposition to change of those habits are the weakest links in efforts to strengthen higher education's response to modern demands. Trustees and others are now urging and even ordering administrators to move in on the faculty in various ways.

As a rather natural consequence of this challenging atmosphere, even the long-standing authority of the faculty to determine the curriculum and the academic requirements is under heavy pressure. Since control of the curriculum is the inner citadel of faculty power, faculty members are becoming increasingly defensive about protecting the citadel. Hence, the whole question of innovation or reform is becoming increasingly suspect.

If anything, faculties during the late 1960s were more open to change than they are now. With their defense mechanisms thoroughly worked up by the aggravated form of the challenge, faculties are stalling and have actually reduced the opportunity for curricular and teaching-learning innovation at the present time.

3. LACK OF SUSTAINED RESOURCES

Unfortunately, most innovative efforts tend, in a budget and manpower sense, to be additive rather than supportive of existing academic programs. Institutions sometimes can find limited funds to start new and interesting programs, but funds to do a better job with existing programs are exceedingly hard to come by. Likewise, even where new programs have been instituted, rarely is enough money provided to see through the changes on a long-term basis. Consequently, in order to get new efforts going and to keep them going, staff and dollars have to be redeployed or "bootlegged" from existing or regular tasks. Much of this simply falls as extra work upon faculties that, in many cases, are already undermanned in terms of reasonable teacher-pupil ratios.

The most common complaint among faculties today is: "How come all the interest in starting up these new things when they don't even give us the money to handle our existing functions in a proper way?"

More and more faculty members resist even talking about innovations or new programs unless the financial and staff support is crystal clear at the outset. Even then, they are resentful that funds seem to be available for entirely new projects and not for existing undermanned activities.

Since the critics of existing higher education teaching-learning practices feel that these practices are inefficient and ineffective, the faculty complaint falls increasingly on deaf ears. Legislators, donors, trustees, and administrators watch educational costs spiral ever upward, and patience with the faculty and their existing practices and patterns grows ever thinner.

Even in the case of new and interesting experiments in curriculum or teaching-learning practices, all too often the lack of sustained supplementary resources does not permit the experiment to be carried forward long enough to produce a meaningful result. Consequently, at the very time when an in-progress experiment should be evaluated in terms of its being adopted as a model for larger-scale efforts, it frequently is found to be in a declining state. Under declining circumstances the best staff members drift off, competent evaluation becomes progressively more difficult or impossible as the innovative team disintegrates, and the project usually winds up in an indeterminate and finally despised state. Sometime later, it is mercifully reorganized out of existence.

For many of these reasons, incredibly few curricular and teaching-learning reform projects are ever systematically or conclusively evaluated; and therefore, they do not form the basis for stimulating imitation or adaptation elsewhere.

4. INNOVA-TION RUNS COUNTER TO THE RHYTHM OF HIGHER EDUCATION

(This point is related to item 3.)

Unfortunately, serious and well-founded innovative efforts require long lead times for conceptualization, development, operation, and finally evaluation. Directly working against the availability of the time required to do all these things is the rhythm of higher education. Faculty members tend to operate largely under national labor market or professional or academic year time factors. They come from and go on sabbaticals or leaves; they change institutions; they take time to work on research projects or books; they do consultant work; or their interests simply change.

All this causes considerable difficulty in fashioning an innovative team and holding it together for more than a year or so. Comparably, most innovative projects these days involve both undergraduate and graduate students. Necessarily, their span of attention on any one thing is very brief as their interests change and as they progress term by term on their academic way.

5. LACK OF FACULTY TIME

Very little of the time of higher education faculties is available for or, indeed, actually spent in creative activity connected with curricular and teaching-learning reform.

Certainly, flashes of inspiration can occur in the minds of even harried individuals, but genuine and meaningful change efforts in higher education require a good deal beyond flashes of inspiration. They require careful thought, preparation, explanation, trial, and evaluation. These creative activities are not merely time-consuming; they require at times nearly total preoccupation. Rarely are such blocks of time available to higher education staff members.

Although many in the outer public do not appreciate the fact, a majority of higher education faculty members, and not just those with administrative responsibilities, are chronically overcommitted from a time standpoint.

In addition to their class time student contact hours, faculty members spend much time preparing for classes, advising students, preparing and correcting tests, reading and judging student papers, and serving on thesis committees.

In addition, most faculty members *try* to keep up with the mountains of reading material related to their interests, and it is an increasingly hopeless task. Many are also carrying on research projects and spend much time in laboratories or on field inspections and surveys.

Then, faculty members have extensive obligations to join in departmental staff work, such as duty on curriculum and personnel search committees; and they must attend departmental staff meetings and, increasingly, meetings of various types with student representatives.

Many faculty members prepare books; criticize proposed books or articles of others; consult with government, industry, or other educational institutions; and travel to and attend professional and other meetings.

Finally, faculty members who are department chairmen or deans, and those who sit on faculty advisory councils, senates, budget committees, student conduct tribunals, etc., spend vast amounts of their available time in meetings, hearings, negotiations, report-writing sessions, and in seeing a steady and growing stream of visitors.

Insofar as many of these faculty leaders are the same ones who would have to play critical leadership or approval roles in initiating, sustaining, and evaluating reform measures, their preoccupation with these other duties has been a major and serious obstacle to meaningful reform of the curriculum and teaching-learning processes in higher education.

Even if some persons are opposed to the ways faculty members spend their time and to some of the value patterns underlying the time distributions, it is still a fact, nevertheless, that, overall, the present higher education system simply does not provide time for or reward meaningful faculty efforts to devise and institute curricular and teaching-learning reform.

The paucity of significant, widespread efforts and results in this area is evidence enough of the problem; and the situation will not change until the system finds ways of providing protected blocks of time for and rewards to the faculty who have a capacity for creative work in curricular and teaching-learning reform.

6. THE LAW OF DRIFTBACK Innovative efforts are like moving objects in that they are subject to accumulated friction.

The more innovative or even revolutionary a new curricular or teaching project may be, the greater is the problem of developing and sustaining forward motion. For many of the reasons above, plus the difficulties of keeping a constantly changing innovative team operating with full effectiveness and understanding, innovative efforts soon become lopsided or unbalanced. Some parts go forward; other parts fall away. Some parts of the team operate effectively, and others poorly.

Cost factors begin to operate against continuing apparently low-benefit parts of an experiment. These factors, plus hiring difficulties, or administrative rigidities or hurdles, tend to slow innovative motion, skew or confuse results, and finally, reduce change action to an almost imperceptible level.

Moreover, new faculty members and the ever-renewing student body become progressively unaware or unappreciative of what was innovative about a program because they are not familiar with what past programs were like. Moreover, they usually bring other or new urgencies with them, and focus on the earlier goals of the project becomes increasingly difficult to maintain.

Gradually, evidence of the innovative effort, like sand castles on the beach, is wiped out, with little or no trace left behind.

In short, unless innovative efforts can maintain a solid thrust, accumulated human and institutional factors will eventually slow them, consume them, and finally, frustrate their purposes.

7. FACULTY RESISTANCE TO CHANGES All of us fall into habits, patterns, and styles in the conduct of our day-to-day work or activities. Resistance to change is probably one of the most common human characteristics. In the case of faculty members, some prefer the basic order and simplicity of relating to students through a stand-up lecture. Others prefer give-and-take sessions in small seminar settings. Obviously, styles are also dictated by conditions where enrollments are heavy and teacher-pupil ratios are high.

The professors tend to adopt whatever style will allow them to function in a satisfactory manner. Concepts of what is satisfactory will tend to vary according to operating conditions. Over time, these patterns or styles, however determined, become habitual, and their day-to-day practice becomes a matter of rhythm and even security to the faculty members involved.

Efforts at curricular or teaching-learning innovation necessarily upset or threaten these operating patterns. They cause rearrangements, and they throw open teacher-pupil relationships. Many of the current innovative efforts directly change the very role of the faculty member, and certainly challenge his undisputed authority in the classroom.

Innovations commonly call for greater initiative to be given to the student in determining his program, and they directly challenge the whole faculty role in establishing requirements for particular academic degrees.

Some few professors welcome changes in matters of style, curriculum content, and classroom procedure; but most others are troubled by what they feel is the evident lack of order, coherence, and integrity in many so-called innovative efforts. Accordingly, they are becoming increasingly resistant, or at least quite conservative, in the business of proposing, participating in, or even considering innovations.

8. LACK OF EXPERIMENTATION BY LEADER INSTITUTIONS OR FACULTY MEMBERS

Even a cursory examination of most of the recent innovative efforts in higher education reveals that the normal leader-type institutions are not the ones pushing highly experimental or innovative efforts. In most cases, the institutions engaging in these activities are relatively small, and in some cases unknown or new institutions. Consequently, even where an experiment may prove to be fairly successful, its impact is nowhere near as great as if the same experiment had been instituted and pushed by a leader institution.

Comparably, on an individual basis, very few of the acknowledged outstanding professors in the nation have taken the lead in creative efforts in curriculum innovation or reform of teaching-learning practices. Although the reasons for this phenomenon are not precisely known, it probably can be explained in terms of one or more of the list of obstacles discussed in this memorandum.

9. LACK OF PROFESSIONAL CONSTITUENCIES FOR INTERDISCIPLINARY EFFORTS

It is a basic characteristic of academic life that faculty members as a group tend to identify first with their professional disciplinary constituencies and organizations. Very few professional organizations exist to backstop, support, or provide recognition for interdisciplinary efforts.

Since many of the innovative experiments necessarily involve attempts to blend disciplinary efforts, they fail to attract or hold for long the solid interest and backing of the specialized constituencies. Faculty members who join in such interdisciplinary efforts often lose a sense of professional home, and even their academic titles are considered nondescript by the specialized disciplinarians. Institutions that seek to hire faculty members for interdisciplinary efforts usually will find the candidates inquiring about the identity insurance of having an academic berth in one of the traditional departments. However, most disciplinary departments tend to favor hiring persons of disciplinary promise who will help carry the disciplinary load. Thus, they prefer not to provide academic homes for part-time staff members who will be preoccupied with other things.

Even the institutions themselves usually fail to reward faculty members for interdisciplinary efforts. This is particularly troublesome in graduate schools where degree candidates who develop interdisciplinary theses have considerable difficulty enlisting the help of faculty advisors or thesis committee members; and disciplinary departments usually prefer that their staff members give first priority to their own disciplinary degree candidates.

10. LACK OF KNOWLEDGE CONCERNING HUMAN LEARNING BEHAVIORS AND STYLES

Possibly a fundamental factor underlying all the above-mentioned obstacles is the lack of faculty knowledge about how and when students really learn.

Incredibly few members of higher education faculties are trained to teach. Even fewer have studied human learning behavior in any systematic way.

Professors are taught their subject matters as students themselves. If they give evidence of the necessary competencies, they are given their graduate degrees. It is then simply presumed that they can teach their subject matter specialties to other people. On the basis of that presumption, they are hired and begin teaching.

Some faculty members do very well at helping people learn. In many of the science disciplines and in some of the professional schools, the students do laboratory work and demonstrate by their activities and behaviors what they have learned. However, in the social sciences and humanities, such laboratory demonstrations are not readily possible. The tendency, therefore, is simply to assume that students are learning, or learning in some measure, because they attend class and test average or better on a given set of questions posed from time to time.

All too often, however, the test questions reveal varying degrees of student competence at memorization and regurgitation of the professor's lectures or the lessons, rather than an ability to make actual functional use of basic ideas and relationships as well as skills of analysis and evaluation. Compounding the lack of effective social science and humanities laboratories is the further difficulty that professors have in being fuzzy or unconcerned about desired learning outcomes for the various parts of their courses. Indeed, many faculty members have not conceptualized how a student who has "learned" what they have "taught" should give evidence of such learning through actual behaviors.

Moreover, faculty members who lack knowledge about desired learning outcomes for their students are not likely to be very innovative in trying a variety of methods over time to check actual student learning results. They simply offer their courses on a take-it-or-leave-it basis, without any particular sense of responsibility for what actually happens to the student.

Even the able professors who keep up to date in their professional areas are more likely to put their emphasis on the accuracy of their content rather than on what student behaviors are really learned or acquired from it.

CONCLUSIONS Obviously, those ambitious to institute and achieve meaningful curricular and teaching-learning reform first must take into account the kinds of obstacles noted above, and then, wherever possible, seek to overcome or at least neutralize as many of them as possible.

Clearly, this would be no small task. However, considering the alarming deterioration of public confidence in the costs, processes, participants, and results of higher education, and considering what is at stake, attempts to overcome these obstacles to reform must be of the highest priority for all elements of higher education, the government, and private philanthropy.

Despite all the signal flags clearly warning "Danger," it is abundantly evident that remedial efforts to correct the weaknesses of higher education are not taking place in the directions and with the speed and on the scale that the situation demands.

However, even though we may warn, criticize, bemoan, or even wail about all the wrong things that characterize higher education or faculty practices, we are not really in a position to simply scrap the system and start anew.

First of all, we really are nowhere near agreement, even partially, on any alternative higher education system to replace the one we have. Therefore, unless we are prepared to risk chaos, we had better concentrate on encouraging a spirit of reform in connection with the existing system.

In particular, we must realize that with all its faults and problems, the faculty component of higher education is a vast national resource. Presently, broad parts of that resource are demoralized, confused, and increasingly defensive and negative. We must find the means for changing these conditions. And this, in turn, will depend upon constructive measures that help change faculty attitudes and values and encourage faculty members to adopt behaviors that facilitate curricular and teaching-learning reform.

Many faculty members concede the weaknesses in both the curricular and teaching-learning systems that they use, but they do not see clear ways to move toward improvements. Quite the contrary, all about them they see a lack of institutional commitment or a lack of adequate resources to facilitate the accomplishment of even those few changes on which there might be agreement.

Thus, those institutions in our society that have a genuine concern for curricular and teaching-learning reform, and particularly those that have the resources to help in these regards, must help find the ways to encourage faculty members to take leadership in developing and testing new ideas and concepts with respect to curricular and teaching-learning systems. We already have many promising ideas, but we lag far behind in instituting and testing these ideas on a sustained basis in order to judge their potential for wide-scale use.

Along this line, special attention should be given to those few projects of curricular and teaching-learning reform that appear to be successful and really meaningful, or are in striking range of being so. They may offer us clues about how those responsible for these projects have contended with, or cut through, the kinds of obstacles described above. Whether or not such successful projects followed principles or concepts that are susceptible of generalization to the broad field of higher education remains to be discovered, but they certainly warrant the closest scrutiny at this time.

Also, since meaningful curricular and teaching-learning reform depends upon changes in faculty values and behaviors, constructive action along this line is not likely to occur if arbitrary, mandatory, and authoritarian tactics are employed to coerce the faculty. More likely, this would only aggravate relationships further and discourage constructive behavior.

Finally, while some people are arguing that the growing crisis of higher education demands prompt and stern measures, the real tests in considering any proposed measures are their soundness as alternatives to present methods and their likely results.

Those who are demanding radical and abrupt change in the curriculum and in teaching-learning practices, and who are demeaning faculty competencies and values, are, by the nature of what they are doing, acting unwisely and unrealistically. In a sense, they are writing off the faculty as a vital part of the reform process.

Yet, as argued above, the faculty is inherently and obviously the key resource we have for leadership, initiative, and know-how in the matter of improving the curriculum and strengthening teaching-learning practices.

For example, the most frequently developed conclusion about individual learning techniques is that "hardware" has gotten ahead of "software." However, "software" has to be produced by the faculty. There is no process of artificial insemination that will cover the kind of faculty creativity and leadership that is needed in developing meaningful programs for use in individual learning situations.

Also, we are hardly likely to make much large-scale progress in the reform of higher education by demanding a sharp break in the pattern of faculty practices and techniques. For instance, whereas we are hopeful that certain of the newer media can become integral parts of teaching-learning systems, we should not despair because professors may be inclined at first merely to adapt their existing course and teaching techniques to these newer media. Quite naturally, they will function best if they feel comfortable in what they are doing, and this will most likely occur if they retain familiar bearings or recognition points.

Then, after faculty members have been helped to develop familiarity and ease in programming their existing course contents with the help of the newer media, they can more readily be encouraged and be given assistance to rethink what they do and what they want to achieve by way of learning outcomes. At that point, with proper help and reinforcement, many faculty members, quite quickly and naturally, will move on to explore fresh curricular and teaching-learning strategies.

Clearly this approach involves painstaking and time-consuming efforts; and such a course may seem unrealistic in terms of today's potential crisis conditions. However, again, the real measure of progress will be what produces actual, beneficial results on a large national scale.

In these key areas of faculty interest, compulsory and arbitrary measures dictated by higher education or other administrative authorities to coerce the faculty into new methodologies or to change their roles and practices in a sharp and abrupt manner are not likely to be productive of constructive results; and, therefore, while they may be argued for in terms of producing quick action, their results, if nonconstructive, would really mean that valuable time and energy would be actually wasted.

These comments apply equally to the notions of some that for economic and quality reasons higher education institutions will have to purchase or rent high-quality course offerings prepared nationally and make them available to their students. It is often suggested that this will be the only way for each institution to avoid investing vast sums in costly technology only to have it used by mediocre local professors "to peddle their own dull stuff."

While some imaginative and innovative ways of presenting course contents may be importable, most professors feel more comfortable with their own adaptations. While they should be encouraged and helped to see how things are done elsewhere, and to discover what new and interesting techniques could be applied to their own efforts, they should in no way be allowed to feel that the administration intends to displace them or to dictate how they should perform their teaching roles.

In short, reforms, if they are to come on a wide enough scale, will have to come mainly as a consequence of local action and leadership on the many campuses around the nation.

While this will take time and we will not always see funds used in the most educationally effective ways, we really do not have a solid, workable alternative way of moving from where we are now to where we would hope to go.

The key lies in motivating the faculty along constructive lines.

What is needed are confirming demonstrations by colleges and universities that encourage and reward a voluntary response from their interested faculty members to join, rejoin, or step up efforts toward strengthening curricular programming and teaching-learning practices. Necessarily, these confirming demonstrations must be supported and sustained until they are able to produce reasonable conclusive results relating to their validity for possible use or adaptation more generally.

With the best will in the world, few higher education institutions are likely to be able to provide the kind of support needed. Substantial and continuing help from government and private philanthropy, therefore, will have to be a vital component in a meaningful action strategy.

Appendix D: A Plan for a College

David Bakan

This plan arises out of a sense that educational reform is acutely needed, combined with no less a sense that the direction of reform must be toward increased academic freedom, where that term means, as it has meant in history, both the *freedom to teach* and the *freedom to learn*. The plan will be presented first, and then commented upon.

THE PLAN
1. Each professor shall offer his course in complete freedom as to its content and the method of instruction.

2. The professor shall make available a description of the course reasonably ahead of the time that the course will be offered.

3. If possible, the course description should identify the course as belonging among the humanities, biological sciences, physical sciences or social sciences.

4. If possible, the course description should identify it as suitable for first year, second year, etc., students.

5. The sixteen categories formed by the four areas of knowledge and the four year levels (e.g., Social Sciences, 3rd year) are to be understood as rough guides to the student, and not binding with respect to his choice of courses.

6. The course description should clearly indicate such proficiencies as may be required for taking the course; and the means that the professor deems suitable for determining these proficiencies. The professor may require the passing of an examination,

NOTE: The material in Appendix D is reprinted with permission from *Canadian University & College*, York University, Toronto, June 1969, pp. 30–34, 42–43.

to be administered prior to the beginning of the course, specific course preparation, or an interview.

7.   The student may take any course that he can qualify for as in 6, above. Normally, one would expect that a student in his first or second year would take four courses, distributed among the four categories in recognition of the need for breadth; and in his third or fourth year, to make selections more narrowly, seeking greater depth, and courses more integrated with each other. (Half-year or one-third year courses are completely feasible under this plan.) Nonetheless, it would be contrary to the idea of the plan to make any specific distribution compulsory. There may well be instances in which such a distribution should not be imposed, as, for example, in the case of the extremely able and well prepared student whose education has already carried him beyond the breadth that an ordinary "distribution-requirement" curriculum might have provided him with. Appropriate advisory services to help the student in both assessing his own characteristics and in selecting courses might be developed as circumstances indicate.

8.   Upon attestation of satisfactory completion of fourteen courses a Bachelor of Arts degree will be awarded.

9.   The actual conduct of a course may be quite conventional; or as unconventional as may appear appropriate. Thus, a professor may hold classes in a conventional two to five scheduled hours a week, or otherwise as indicated by the subject matter and characteristics of the students involved.

10.   The professor shall hold at least *three individual tutorial hours* with the student in which the following functions will be served:

a   In the first prescribed tutorial hour, the professor and the student shall agree to the student's assignment for the course. This assignment shall deal with attendance at lectures (which may include lectures by other professors), readings, writings, such other things as they may mutually agree upon, and a schedule for completing the assignment. The professor may, if he so chooses, require some exercises and a minimum reading schedule necessary for effective work in the course for all the students in it; and, of course, vary it in accordance with the preparation and aims of the student. One would think, for example, that in basic language and mathematics courses the nature of the assignment would be largely determined by the professor. In courses in literature or philosophy one might expect greater exercise of the student's prerogative in designing the assignment. Similar assignments for several individuals in a course may be worked out, to form sub-groups in the course. What is often called a "reading course" can readily be worked in under the proposed structure simply by designing the assignment appropriately. The assignment thus agreed upon shall be in writing.

b   In the second prescribed tutorial hour, a review of the student's progress shall be made. At this time the assignment will be reviewed and modified if desirable.

c   In the third prescribed tutorial hour, the professor shall determine whether the assignment has been satisfactorily completed. If he judges that the student has satisfactorily completed the assignment, he shall make an attestation to that effect for the student's permanent record. Should he judge that the assignment has not been satisfactorily completed there shall be no entry in the student's permanent record.

11.   For each course (or part-course) thus satisfactorily completed there shall be a permanent record for the student containing the following:

a   The title and description of the course.

b   A vita on the professor.

c   The agreed-upon assignment.

d   The professor's attestation of satisfactory completion of that assignment.

This need be nothing more than a formal statement such as: "In my opinion John Doe has satisfactorily completed the assignment described above."

The plan does not preclude the use of examinations as a teaching aid; nor does it preclude the professor's use of examination to help him to decide whether to make an attestation of satisfactory performance. Indeed, the passing of an examination might be written into the assignment. However, this permanent record shall contain no letter or numerical grades, or any form of evaluation or assessment of level of performance as in a conventional permanent record. *It should not be confused with Pass-Fail grading system.* If the student has not satisfactorily completed the assignment there would simply be no entry in the permanent record.

THE COST OF THE PLAN   At first glance it may appear that such highly individualized instruction as the plan conceives of would be very expensive. In order to show its financial feasibility consider a hypothetical college with 1,000 students, with, say, 600 students in the freshman and sophomore years, and 400 in the junior and senior years. As the table shows this would entail a minimum number of tutorial hours of 10,800, and 3,600 registrations.

No. of students	Courses per student	Minimum tutorial hours per course	Tutorial hours	Regis- trations
600	4	3	7,200	2,400
400	3	3	3,600	1,200
			10,800	3,600

With a faculty of 60, this would amount to 180 tutorial hours for each professor (10,800 ÷ 60).

The number of registrations per faculty member would be 60.

If, say, a professor were to give 90 hours a year to meeting with a class in a course—it is rarely this large in a conventional course—then his total contact time with students would be as follows, depending on the number of different courses he teaches.

Number of courses taught	Number of students in course	Class time	Tutorial time	Total con- tact time
1	60	90	180	270
2	30, 30	180	180	360
3	20, 20, 20	270	180	450

The table is hardly to suggest that educational time be subjected to a cost-accounting approach. Yet it reveals that in this plan contact hour time is less than generally current demands on professorial time. For in this very onerous college, with an extremely high student-teacher ratio (almost 17 to 1) and a 30-week teaching year, minimum contact time has an outside limit of 15 contact hours per week (450/30 = 15). So onerous a teaching load existed during the worst years of the depression among academic institutions. Thus, the plan would certainly be financially feasible for any academic institution in which the student-teacher ratio is already less than 17:1. I should stress that I am hardly advocating such a large ratio. I have chosen this hypothetical example as an extreme to show that it would be feasible even in colleges which already have heavily overworked faculties.

Although the plan as outlined calls for a minimum of three tutorial hours, this should not be taken to indicate that three is anything but a minimum. One would hope that an educational enterprise such as that which has been outlined, in which a critical feature is that it shall be fueled by interest of faculty and students, would entail voluntary association in connection with the educational enterprise. And certainly we could presume that the smaller the student-teacher ratio would be, the more excellent would the educational experience tend to be and the greater the degree of such voluntary association.

If, in this hypothetical college, each professor were to teach only one course, there would be 60 courses from which the students could choose. With 60 professors each teaching one course only, there would be an average of almost 4 courses in each of the sixteen area-year categories. Even in such a small college there would be reasonable diversity. The larger the school the greater would be the possibilities.

IMPROVING THE QUALITY OF EDUCATION BY MEANS OF THE PLAN It would be hoped that one of the important benefits of putting the plan into effect would be the improvement of instruction through the encouragement of teachers *to teach that which they are competent to teach and that which they are interested in.* A major factor responsible for the poor teaching that goes on at colleges and universities is that teachers are often forced to teach what they are not prepared to teach or what they are not interested in. Most of the time the planning of curricula is not done by the identical personnel who teach those curricula. At any rate, curricula are commonly *collectively* planned, while the teaching is done by individuals. In the plan which has been outlined the person *who* is to teach is the person who determines *what* he is to teach.

The common rhetoric these days in finding a professor for a course starts with the need for someone to teach a course that is "on the books." The existence of courses on the books, especially if they are required, is one of the most frequently used arguments by department chairmen for justifying new appointments. Having received the budgetary allotment for such a new appointment, the chairman must then find someone to teach *that* course, and not necessarily one that the new appointee may be more qualified to teach. The new appointee, filled with a sense that teaching that particular course is "the job," does what he can in all honesty and integrity. Often he feels inadequate to it and less than fully interested in it. The result is that he presents an image to the students, no matter how good an actor he is or how conscientious he may be, of at least relative incompetence in the subject matter and relative lack of interest in it. The cynicism that can arise in both professors and students under these circumstances is unfortunately part of the general experience of many.

The situation is particularly acute in connection with younger teachers. A person who has recently acquired a Ph.D. is characteristically one who has recently devoted himself to the intense investigation of some limited area of knowledge. His first teaching position generally involves teaching the general field as an introductory course in the subject. The necessity for teaching the whole field makes him, at best, somewhat more competent than many of his students, and often, less competent than some of his better students; since all that may divide student from teacher is mastery of a single text-book. Needless to say, his inadequacy with respect to the subject matter, combined with the usual insecurity that a young teacher may feel in his authority, hardly work to make the educational experience of the student a good one. The teacher himself soon learns to seek progress in his own academic career by avoiding teaching as much as circumstances allow.

I believe that the almost universal desire to have lower teaching "loads" is associated with a general sense of the tastelessness of the teaching enterprise because of poor initial experiences. It has led in a great many places to turning the bulk of the teaching enterprise over to persons who are relatively professionally immature. This, in turn, of course, leads to a new generation of persons who would again leave the teaching enterprise as soon as possible, again turning it over to the junior people, perpetuating a vicious system. (I have often suspected that even the "publish or perish" mentality in academia is supported by the simple fact that persons who make judgments on others are so often persons who themselves have been traumatized in their teaching experiences and who thus find criteria other than teaching more commendable than a balanced view would suggest.)

Under the plan proposed here the professor will teach what he is competent to teach; or at any rate what he would adventure to learn himself. One would hope that a good deal of the cynicism associated with education might thus be replaced with interest and even passion with respect to the subject matter.

The "large course" has emerged in recent years as a popular form of organization. It is often a required course for large numbers of freshmen or sophomores. Typically, in such a "large course" the several hundred, or even thousands, of students gather in a large auditorium for what is usually a weekly lecture. Then they meet in smaller groups or sections with an individual instructor. Mostly the readings for the course are standard across all of the sections; and mostly there is a common examination for the course. This particular system has been associated with some of the worst features of modern higher education: incompetence on the part of the instructors in the particular material, chopped up and unintegrated sets of readings, ambiguity, with respect to both student and teacher responsibility, unreasonable grading procedures, and great frustration on the part of both students and faculty.

The "large course" is often justified as an expression of "team teaching" or an "inter-disciplinary" approach. Certainly the idea of team teaching, especially in the modern intellectual world where ideally we might be seeking interdisciplinary approaches to our various problems, is attractive. Under the plan which has been outlined it would be possible and desirable for several professors to work out a plan for the handling of a number of students equal to the sum of their individual registration responsibilities. But this should be based completely on *voluntary commitment* of these professors emerging out of some happy confluence of interests, rather than on the basis of structural demand; and it should exist only as long as it furthers a better educational experience for the students and faculty involved.

It would be hoped that the plan would work toward overcoming the felt incompatibility between teaching and research, that is so much the experience of many college professors. For whereas the direction of the professor's research follows the inner logic of the problem that he is working on, the direction of his teaching is often based on shabby educational considerations in which he may even have had no part of the decision. A critic might say that the plan would encourage a professor to proceed quite autistically in his teaching enterprise, without any consideration of the needs of students. The fact of the matter is that there already exists a good deal of autistic teaching and that conventional planned curricula provide no guarantees against that. Indeed, the consequence of the plan would be to make it easier for the student to identify such autistic teaching than in conventional plans. One would also think that if the professor has any educational conscience at all he would attempt to present the things that he is interested in, in ways cognizant of the needs and interests of students. It has been said that the ideal scholar or research worker is one who, having done his work, is filled with the desire to tell someone about it; the latter being what publication should be. It would be hoped that under this plan, some of that need on the part of scholars and research workers might be satisfied by the eager young people sitting in the classrooms.

The plan meets one of the most frequently arising modern criticisms of education, the debasement of education through impersonality. The plan provides that *no matter how large the college or the university shall grow, the integrity of the fundamental unit, the relationship between a student and professor, shall be protected.* Those who would excuse the occurrence of this growing impersonality argue that the large numbers of students make it necessary. In the example which was cited above, I used a hypothetical college of 1,000 students with 60 faculty, giving a ratio of almost 17 to 1. Such a ratio is in fact characteristic only of the poorest of colleges. At some of the wealthier academies the ratio is often less than 10:1. Yet, even at some of the great universities, where the ratio is low, the problems of lack of contact between professor and student, of impersonality in the educational enterprise, of poor teaching, are still acute. The most competent people are characteristically unavailable to the students on a personal basis. Mostly, very junior people might be available, but often in contexts of material which they are not quite competent to teach. The required minimal three hours of tutorial time of the plan at least guarantees that the professor gets to know the student personally in the educational context. In one major university that I know, a common complaint of undergraduates when they reach the senior year and wish to go on to graduate school is that there is no one who knows them well enough to be able to write a letter of recommendation on their behalf to graduate schools.

The plan should work to encourage the student to teach himself. In the modern world the hope would be that education is a process that continues throughout the life of the individual. In this plan, even though the student would get more personal attention in the tutorial hours, the design and conduct of the educational program moves onto the shoulders of the students as rapidly as he can assume it. One of the main defects of conventional education is that the student learns to take his educational assignments almost exclusively from others. Ironically, it is too often the case that the "good" student is the one who least tries to guide his own education.

The plan allows for great flexibility in fashioning a program of studies. The student can, if he so wishes, pace his education so that it could be either less than or greater than the ordinary four years. A student who wishes to accelerate can program his time and assignments so as to use the whole calendar rather than the shorter academic calendar to fulfill the assignments. The student who wishes to extend the period to five or six years or longer may readily do so. It would be completely feasible for a student to integrate work and money earning into his academic program.

THE INTE-GRATION OF EDUCATION IN THE PLAN One of the seeming objections that may be levelled against the plan which is being proposed is that it fails to provide the student with a coordinated educational experience. The old idea of a college curriculum presumed that there was a designable body of knowledge associated with our civilization which could somehow be encompassed, even if very sketchily, in a four year period for reasonably intelligent young people. However, the situation has changed. The world of relevant knowledge has become so vast, the knowledge explosion has become so great, that the most valuable form of education is that which develops in the students as Richard M. Jones has put it, "the intellectual and emotional wherewithal for gaining access to new knowledge."*

The idea of an organized relatively complete curriculum informed by a vision of the presumptive organization of the knowledge possessed by mankind must fail simply because it is unrealistic. Let us consider the argument that there should be coordination of the educational offerings simply on pedagogical grounds. Here we are presented with two principal reasons as to why the relationships among courses that a student takes should be planned and integrated. The first is that there are some things which simply cannot be learned without first reaching certain levels of proficiency. For example, a course in French literature would be inappropriate for students who have not already learned to read French sufficiently well to read that literature; or, a student cannot learn calculus until he has reached a certain level of competence in algebra. This particular need for integration has been met in the plan by giving the professor the prerogative of specifying admission requirements for the course, including an examination.

*Richard M. Jones (ed.): *Contemporary Educational Psychology,* Harper & Row, Publishers, Inc., New York, 1967, p. 187.

The second reason that validates curriculum planning is the desirability of having diversity; that a student should not go through college without some vision of the breadth of man's intellectual probings. The plan which has been outlined certainly would tend to achieve diversity. One can be quite sure that if each faculty member is allowed and encouraged to teach that which he is genuinely interested in, diversity of offerings will follow. In addition, the plan has also added an encouragement to the student to do some sampling from each of the major sub-areas of knowledge. One would hope that under the plan the student would feel foolish should he allow himself to graduate without, say, some broad exposure to the humanities and the sciences. There certainly might be some few cases of students who would wish to take no courses except those they deemed directly equipping them for a career, say, in chemistry. Even such as those, however, might be persuaded that they would be better equipped for executive positions with some knowledge of sociology and political science, more attractive candidates as trustees of cultural institutions with some knowledge of the humanities, better able to deal with the chemistry of drugs with some knowledge of biology, and more likely to be effective in communication with courses in English and foreign languages.

Aside from these two reasons for the deliberate regulation of curricula there lurks a third, more energetic but less noble. This is the personal presumption on the part of many academics that they *know what a student should know.* Unfortunately few really know what one should know. What in point of fact happens is that professors come to feel that what they happen to know (or aspire to know, and don't — in which case they become all the more adamant) is what a student ought to know. The corruption to which this presumption leads is that curricular planning becomes political struggle among disciplines for "representation." This is particularly likely when matters of budget are associated with the outcomes of these political struggles. The struggles of committees, which consume great amounts of time (and hence great portions of the educational budget), are too often based more on academic political considerations than on the educational needs of the students.

The programs which emerge out of these political struggles among professors for a place in the sun of the curriculum, as it were, for their particular disciplines characteristically fail to provide the very integration which might justify the effort in the first place. The programs tend to be political treaties and compromises rather than integrations. Sometimes they result in educational experiences which are disastrously chopped up, which lack any intrinsic integration, which provide the student with a kaleidoscopic vision of the knowledge enterprise, and which deprive him of the opportunity of getting interested in anything. Too often the situation justifies a remark once made to me by a student, "The art of being a good student is in not letting yourself get too interested in anything."

In contrast, for example, under the plan a student who intends to go into the ministry might make a meaningful integration for himself by registering simultaneously in a course in *The Bible as Literature, Ancient History, Hebrew* and perhaps *The Psychology of Adolescence;* combined with a summer on a Kibbutz in Israel to fulfill his assignment in Hebrew; rather than four courses agreed upon in a treaty among competing professors.

GRADES AND QUALITY OF EDUCATION

Perhaps the most radical feature of the plan is the elimination of any permanent record of relative performance such as grades or even pass-fail (which is a grading system of two categories). It is this feature of the plan which would appear to need the greatest defense in view of the central and critical place that grading has in virtually every college in the world.

There are two reasons generally offered to legitimate the use of grades in a college program. The first is that the grading serves to enhance the quality of the educational experience. The second is that grades are essential advisory pieces of information in connection with future educational and vocational decisions. I will deal with these in turn.

If grades are to be considered to be of value in enhancing the quality of education, then the examinations on which they are characteristically based should appropriately measure what they presume to measure. There are numerous criticisms which may be cited to show that such grades based on conventional examinations are actually very poor indices of the relevant traits in the students.

To the best of my knowledge there exist no explicit and generally acceptable guide lines for the assignment of grades. The "curve" was developed some years ago by the psychologist Max Meyer as a way of making grades "objective." The "curve" provides for the assignment of grades in terms of relative performance of students, with a designated percentage getting A, another designated percentage getting B, etc. This atrocity, in minimal fairness, requires that there be a relatively large group of students all subjected to the same educational experiences and provided with the same educational opportunities. It systematically ignores variation from group to group. It assumes that the average of any one large group is identical to the average of any other large group. It assumes that the amount of variation among students in any large group is identical to the amount of variation among students in any other large group. It is systematically blind to the fact that the *quality of instruction varies.* Indeed, *one of the major defects of virtually every grading system is the attribution of variation in quality of performance to the student only, ignoring other factors which may be associated with the performance.*

The trend towards the increased use of "objective" examinations of the multiple-choice and true-false type has not abated. It has been the growing accompaniment of the use of large classes. Such examinations require an inordinately high degree of skill in their construction, for even moderately appropriate evaluation of students; and such skill is rare among college professors. The value of such tests as an educational experience is very doubtful; and they generate a vision of the use of knowledge which is quite inconsistent with many of the values that a liberal education should represent.

In the plan which has been outlined there is a formal place for examination as qualification for admission to a course. But this use of examination is so particular that it escapes many of the usual criticisms. As a qualification for a particular mathematics class the professor may want the student to know how to solve, say, a series of simultaneous equations, since that will be used in some further work; and the professor does not want to take the time of the course to teach that. Or a professor may want to feel free to allude to the content of some particular book, and may want to determine whether the student has mastered the content of that book in a manner sufficient for the purposes that he has at hand.

What effect does grading have on the very quality of the educational enterprise? Were a grading system reasonably reliable and valid it could give the student what psychologists have come to call "knowledge of results," information concerning learning efforts as a basis for improving them. The multiple choice examination can hardly do this. Grades on essay examinations, with their intrinsic unreliability, can hardly do this. If the professor were only the teacher and perhaps even a friendly critic, but not the judge, an examination of any kind might be the occasion for dialogue between them, and thus for the furtherance of the educational enterprise. But, when the professor is equally the judge, placing a grade on a permanent record, such dialogue between the student and the professor is cheapened and the advantage lost by the sensed possibility that they are merely haggling and bickering for ends quite outside the educational enterprise itself.

Grades, instead of producing positive motivation, may create instead hopelessness, apathy, and cynicism. The world is filled with people who carry permanent and unnecessary psychological scars from their youthful experiences with grades and whose effectiveness as adults was made less rather than more. Whether, in balance, the effect of grade pressure is to increase the level of achievement rather than decrease it is quite open to question.

Conventional grading systems work against true cooperation among students in the educational enterprise. When a student is given a grade in comparison with his fellow students, each student who might be superior to him is his "enemy." The professor who is burdened with the task of giving each of his students a separate grade is loathe to make assignments which involve genuine teamwork. In view of the fact that so much of the work of the modern world cannot be done without teamwork, the state of mind created by the grading system may handicap a student from performing effectively in later years.

Grades play a role, I believe, in the great contemporary crisis that exists between students and professors. Grades have come to play an extremely important role in the last few decades in connection with admission to schools and admission to various career lines. With this growth of the significance of grades with respect to admission to educational opportunities, career, and even life or death in some cases as where grades were used for draft deferment, that which has played only a small role has taken on very great importance in the total educational enterprise. The degradation to which the grading system can come in contemporary contexts was made very clear to me at the time when grades were being used by the Selective Service Boards to determine which students should get educational deferments. I was witness to students deliberately failing examinations because, as one student told me, getting a good grade might actually mean that he was sending someone else to his death.

The literal power of professor over student has become so large that there is a real question as to whether its very enormity does not now defeat its original purposes. If one agrees to this, it is then reasonable to drop the whole grading enterprise. Grading has outgrown its usefulness for its major function, which was to serve the education of the student. With this new power, exercised by the professor in his giving of grades, the professor is made less of the professional rendering educational services to the students and more the instrument of other agencies. Gradually and even insidiously the professor has been changed from serving students into a kind of personnel officer for other agencies. Frequently, grades are given not only in terms of the actual learning and performance of the student academically, but is influenced by the professor's judgment of the "suitability" of the person for, say, a particular profession, sometimes based on ignoble motives that he or a professional group may have. Awareness of the way in which the increased judicial function, in this sense, of the college professor has come to interfere with his educational function has led, in some instances, to an effort towards the severe separation of the judicial function from the educational function as at the University of Chicago some years ago, in which a separate testing office was established. However, the experience of the last few years indicates rather strongly that the only way in which the educational function may be cleared of the corruption resulting from the exaggerated judicial functions is for the college to drop its judicial function in connection with the education of students.

The modern student is often quite confused. He has come to regard his own freedom as an inalienable right. He has come, perhaps in his idealism, to expect the university to be both an agent and a locus for the fullest exercise of freedom. Yet he often finds himself bound by meaningless and often arbitrarily and mindlessly assigned educational chores which he is told he must fulfill. And much too often, instead of finding professors who allow themselves the freedom of thought that their position especially allows them, finds instead men bound by nameless insecurities and intimidations which are both self-created and mutually supported.

The clear awareness that the professor is no longer the student's "friend" anymore, that the professor is working as the agent of other interests than that of the student, combined with the increased necessity of winning the professor's good will in order to make career progress is, in my opinion, one of the major reasons for the rising bitterness of students the world over. When one person has such great power over another, the latter must have some recourse against incompetence and irresponsibility in the former's exercise of that power. If there is no such recourse available then at the very least the latter needs some assurance that the former is morally meticulous in his exercise of power. Recent events in the history of the world have too many times raised the question of such moral meticulousness on the part of professors and administrators.

References

American Association of University Professors: *Bulletin,* vol. 56, no. 2, June 1970.

Bakan, David: "A Plan for a College," *Canadian University & College,* York University, Toronto, June 1969.

Becker, Gary S.: *Human Capital,* National Bureau of Economic Research, New York, 1964.

Bowen, Howard R.: "The Corporation and the Campus: Corporate Support of Higher Education in the 1970s." *Proceedings of the Academy of Political Science,* vol. XXX, no. 1, 1970, pp. 75–93.

Bowen, Howard R.: *The Finance of Higher Education,* Carnegie Commission on Higher Education, Berkeley, Calif., 1968.

Clapp, Vernon W., and Robert T. Jordan: "Quantitative Criteria for Adequacy of Academic Library Collections," *College and Research Libraries,* vol. 26, September 1965, pp. 371–380.

Computers in Higher Education, Report of the President's Science Advisory Committee, U.S. Government Printing Office, February 1967.

Jenny, Hans H., and G. Richard Wynn: *The Golden Years: A Study of Income and Expenditure Growth and Distribution of 48 Private Four-year Liberal Arts Colleges 1960–1968,* The College of Wooster, 1971.

Kieffer, Jarold A.: "Toward a System of Individually Taught Courses," *Liberal Education,* October 1970.

Ruml, Beardsley, with Donald H. Morrison: *Memo to a College Trustee: A Report on Financial and Structural Problems of the Liberal Arts College,* McGraw-Hill Book Company, New York, 1959.

University of California, Office of the President: "Faculty Effort and Output Study," memorandum for meeting of members of the Committee on Educational Policy, January 15, 1970.

U.S. Office of Education: *Financial Statistics of Higher Education,* January 1969.

U.S. Office of Education: *Higher Education Finances,* June 1968.

*This book was set in Vladimir by University Graphics,
Inc. It was printed on permanent paper and bound by The
Maple Press Company. The designers were Elliot Epstein
and Edward Butler. The editors were Herbert Waentig and
Laura Givner for McGraw-Hill Book Company and Verne A.
Stadtman for the Carnegie Commission on Higher Education.
Frank Matonti and Alice Cohen supervised the production.*